Nova Scotia Cooking

Charles Lief and Heather MacKenzie

KEY PORTER BOOKS

Canadian Cataloguing in Publication Data

Lief, Charles
        Nova Scotia cooking

Includes index.
ISBN 1-55013-916-9

1. Cookery, Canadian – Nova Scotia style. 2. Cookery –
Nova Scotia. I. MacKenzie, Heather (Heather Corrine).
II. Title.

TX715.6.L54   1997   641.59716   C97-931314-7

The publisher gratefully acknowledges the support of the
Canada Council for the Arts and the Ontario Arts Council
for its publishing program.

THE CANADA COUNCIL | LE CONSEIL DES ARTS
FOR THE ARTS | DU CANADA
SINCE 1957 | DEPUIS 1957

For additional information on the
Taste of Nova Scotia program, contact:
Taste of Nova Scotia Society
P.O. Box 368
Truro, Nova Scotia
B2N 5L5

Design: Peter Maher
Illustrations: Elizabeth Owen

Key Porter Books Limited
70 The Esplanade
Toronto, Ontario
Canada M5E 1R2

Printed and bound in Canada

97 98 99 00 6 5 4 3 2 1

DEDICATION

In the late 1980s, a small group of chefs and restaurant owners met with representatives of the Nova Scotia Departments of Tourism, Fisheries and Agriculture. The result of that meeting was the founding of the Taste of Nova Scotia Society in 1989, dedicated to the rediscovery of the rich culinary heritage of our province's indigenous local food products, and the inspiration behind this book and our previous one: *The Taste of Nova Scotia Cookbook.*

Alex Clavel, the Swiss-born chef/owner of the highly regarded Chez La Vigne Restaurant in Wolfville, N.S., was a central figure at that meeting. A living legend in Nova Scotia, Alex began his training as a chef in 1948 and by 1954 was already demonstrating his considerable talent in Toronto and Montreal. Happily for us, he moving to Nova Scotia in 1956. Alex has extraordinary curiosity, and for the past 41 years has traveled the province, meeting with farmers and fishermen, home cooks and restaurant owners, always looking for recipes that use the wonderful ingredients found locally. Alex's idea, that such dishes would appeal to the tourist as well as to local residents, became the founding vision for Taste of Nova Scotia. Chez La Vigne pioneered the presentation of a marvelous variety of these menus winning Alex countless loyal patrons, numerous awards and commendations and a permanent place in the culinary history of Nova Scotia. He is renowned as a teacher of young chefs and an enthusiastic spokesman for the beauty of our province.

We dedicate this book to you, Alex, with gratitude and appreciation. May you continue to inspire us with your wit and wisdom.

CONTENTS

ACKNOWLEDGMENTS

How gratifying it was to see our first cookbook, *The Taste of Nova Scotia*, in print and on the bookstore shelves. When it became a Canadian bestseller, we realized that our mission to share the tradition of Nova Scotia cuisine with a wide audience had succeeded. We hope that the readers of *Nova Scotia Cooking* will enjoy these new recipes and stories.

The member of restaurants of the Taste of Nova Scotia Society, and especially the board of directors, were a constant source of creative ideas and encouragement. We are also grateful for the support provided by the Nova Scotia Department of Agriculture and Marketing, the Nova Scotia Department of Fisheries and Aquaculture and the Nova Scotia Commodity Group. The recipes were expertly tested by Debbie Creelman and Ruth Smith.

We continue to enjoy our relationship with all at Key Porter Books, and particularly thank Barbara Berson for her skilled editing and Susan Renouf and Anna Porter for their enthusiastic support.

Our families—Judy, Jessica and Deborah Lief and Les, Joanna and Craig MacKenzie—need to be thanked again. After living through the creation of the first book, they actually encouraged us to do it again.

INTRODUCTION

Nova Scotians love a celebration. It's no wonder that each year, hundreds of fairs and festivals take place across the province, giving neighbors a chance to catch up on the news and visitors the best opportunity to partake of the exceptionally friendly Nova Scotia hospitality. The common thread running through these events is food. Fresh fruits and vegetables for sale, apple or berry pies entered into contests, a simple, delicious lobster sandwich on homemade bread at the refreshment stand, or a table laden with maple syrup, sugar and candy—all are locally made, direct from the sea or the farm and marvelous to eat. It is from this simple, "old-fashioned" experience that this book originates. We look to the food history of the province, at the locally produced ingredients and the wonderful—and wonderfully creative—dishes made from those ingredients. This relationship, between producer and cook, defines "regional cuisine."

The culinary world understands that food which travels the shortest possible distance from source to table has the fullest flavor. Nova Scotia is blessed with farmers and fishermen who produce the best, in a place small enough for the products to get to the kitchen quickly. Skilful home cooks have always made use of local ingredients for delicious family meals, developing a repertoire of traditional recipes over hundreds of years. As cities grew and tourists arrived, chefs with vision looked to those old traditional recipes as the inspiration for new ones.

Food production and preparation has played an important role in Nova Scotia for the past 380 years, longer than anywhere else in Canada. French colonists started the first farms in Port Royal, Nova Scotia, in 1606, followed quickly by orchards. Acadians, as the French settlers were known, were used to reclaiming low lying, marshy land on the French Atlantic coast and were well suited to the struggle of keeping dry farmland and the high tides of the Bay of Fundy in their respective places. The early farmers grew grains, potatoes, onions, turnips, carrots, beans, corn, pumpkin, all suitable for winter storage either as is or preserved. They also raised dairy cows, sheep, goats and poultry. Woodlands surrounding the farms yielded fiddleheads, dandelion greens, wild berries, mushrooms, incredible maple syrup as well as wild turkey, pheasant and other game. Fishermen landed tremendous catches of shellfish—lobster, scallops, mussels and oysters—along with salmon, trout, haddock, halibut, herring and cod. Food not eaten right away was dried, pickled or canned for the winter. Excess milk and cream went into cheese and some of the fruit became homemade wine or sweet preserves.

Fundamentally, nothing has changed. The basic crops and catches are much the same. Of course, the ancestors probably didn't grow radicchio or make salsa for the pantry, but the skill of the grower and the creativity of the cook have made them possible. Environmental pressures have challenged the farmer and the abundant fish stocks have been seriously threatened. Happily, much is happening to reestablish the sustainable family farm and the fishery. The organic movement is finding a home in Nova Scotia. Conservation of the threatened fish species is a serious program now showing promising results.

There is nothing unique about the food we produce in Nova Scotia. These same foods can be found in New England, the northwest of Canada or the United States or northern Europe. What is special is the way in which the foods are used, the recipes that have been saved over the generations and the new ones that have drawn upon the past. Local history and culture combines the cook, the ingredients and the diner in a mutual celebration that evokes the uniqueness of Nova Scotia as much as does hearing the bagpipe or glimpsing a tartan. This book is in part a historical record. There are many recipes that would be totally familiar to the great cooks of many generations ago. Seafood Stew, Baked Beans, Scotch Barley Broth, Stewed Rhubarb and Apple Dumplings would have been at home on the kitchen table of 300 years ago. *Nova Scotia Cooking* is also meant to show the evolution of the cooking profession, by exploring new ways of using locally produced ingredients. Oven Poached Salmon with Yogurt Dill Sauce, Grilled Chicken and Spinach Salad and Ginger Pear Beets may be new, but somehow familiar to Grandmother's generation.

In writing this book, we asked chefs, farmers, fishermen and ordinary lovers of food for recipes and ideas. The contributions of the member restaurants and chefs of the Taste of Nova Scotia program are as invaluable to *Nova Scotia Cooking* as they were to our first book, *The Taste of Nova Scotia*.

Please have fun with this book in your kitchen. Follow the recipes as we have recorded them—and feel free to improvise. Use fresh ingredients as much as possible. Be prepared to change the menu if some wonderful, fresh product that wasn't part of your meal plan appears in the market. Seasons are short—take advantage. Plan a trip to our province, and discover the kind of food and hospitality that inspired *Maclean's* magazine to call Nova Scotia "the last best place." We agree wholeheartedly.

CHAPTER ONE

LOBSTER, CRAB AND SHRIMP

While Americans may equate Nova Scotia with its smoked salmon, the Bluenosers at home consider the lobster to be the great seafood offering. ("Bluenoser," for the uninitiated, is a term of endearment for Nova Scotia residents; it comes from the sailing ship *Bluenose*, the provincial maritime symbol.) Lobstering has been the source of employment for generations of fishing families who settled the wonderful fishing villages around the circumference of the "almost an island" province. More than a way of making a living, the lobster fishery has defined a way of life for these families. The life is hard and, despite the regal price often commanded by the lobster, the wages are modest. It is an industry that has kept in touch with the past. Even the large distributors today rely heavily on the families that hold the lobster licenses and provide the catch for the voracious market.

Northern Atlantic lobster is renowned as the finest in the world. There is a rivalry between Nova Scotia and Maine for the "best of the best" title, but even the most experienced chef finds the distinction imperceptible. Lobsters are sold in a variety of sizes, and both male and females are marketed. The female often contains coral, the egg sac, which is a delicacy, in addition to the fine white meat. While there are a variety of recipes that use lobster as the basis for complex dishes, the simple method of boiling and eating with a minimum of fussy ingredients (a little butter, or tossed cold with homemade mayonnaise) is the way to truly appreciate how remarkable this ungainly crustacean is. Many older Nova Scotians remember when lobster was so abundant it was considered a poor person's food. Whole lobsters were used as fertilizer on the farms that dot the coastline, and children were embarrassed to take lobster sandwiches to school.

The MacQueens have been fishing the waters off the coast of Cape Breton Island for all of this century. James MacQueen, now 60, has been fishing for 47 years. At 13, he began rowing the boat used by his father, John, to fish lobster. While James rowed, his father would haul the traps up by hand. Following a morning of rowing around Mira Bay, James would walk the four miles (2.5 km) to Mira Gut and help with a tour boat sailing on the Mira River.

The lobster fishery is divided into seasons. License holders are allowed to fish within a specified district for one season lasting several months. As with most lobstermen, the off season was the time to use the boats to land groundfish—cod, haddock, halibut, mackerel and others—and to rebuild and repair the boats, nets and traps. The MacQueens hired a variety of local men, including the boyfriends of James's four daughters, to net the groundfish. John led this crew until he stopped fishing sometime after his 75th birthday.

During the season, James fishes six days a week. The day begins at 4:00 a.m. with breakfast that his wife, Jean, laid out the night before—cereal and fruit, homemade cake or pie—washed down by steaming hot, strong tea. The tea also fills two large thermoses that accompany James on the boat, along with a big packed lunch. For James, lobstering is a solitary occupation, with his son-in-law the only helper. By 5:00 a.m. the two of them are on board the 43-foot (13-m) Cape Islander called the *Daniel and Dennis* after the youngest of the eight grandchildren. James built the fiberglass-hulled boat himself.

Once at sea, James hauls up the 275 traps he is permitted to set. Once the lobsters that meet the size limits are removed and the undersized ones returned to the ocean, more bait is added and the traps returned to the bottom. James traps both the larger "market" size lobsters (a pound and a quarter [560 g] or up) and the "canners" (one pound [450 g]). Canners are called "chicks " in much of the rest of the world, but canners or "shacks" by Nova Scotians. By 3:00 p.m. the *Daniel and Dennis* is back in port, and the work of getting the lobsters to the broker, loading bait for the next day and fueling up takes another couple of hours.

James likes his lobster prepared simply and eaten freshly cooked. He might use melted butter or some vinegar, and eat a bit of potato salad and a fresh roll with it, but that is about it. (Last year he tried "surf and turf" and does admit that a good steak is not a bad accompaniment to the lobster.) Lobster suppers and festivals are some of the most popular social activities to be found in rural Nova Scotia. These events are the way in which communities of neighbors and friends gather to share their unique heritage.

Lobster is not the only crustacean trapped by the Nova Scotia fisherman. Once the lobster season is over, James MacQueen, along with many of his colleagues, go for the crab. The process is different. Lobsters are trapped within sight of shore, but the crab traps are set 25 or 30 miles (40 or 48 km) out to sea. The day begins at 2:30 a.m. and lasts until at least 4:00 in the afternoon. Ever resourceful, James MacQueen told us that he has also purchased a herring license to further extend the season on the water after crab season closes. With such focus and determination, it is clear that the family heritage of earning a living from the sea is likely to be maintained.

LOBSTER BISQUE

Lobster bisque, a smooth, elegant soup, is a traditional New Year's Eve treat for many Nova Scotians.

For those who do not wish to store or cook live lobsters, many fishmarkets sell cooked lobster in the shell, or cans of good quality lobster meat.

2 tbsp	butter	25 mL
1	small onion, chopped	1
2 tbsp	chopped celery	25 mL
2 tbsp	all-purpose flour	25 mL
1½ cups	whole milk or light cream	375 mL
1 cup	chicken stock	250 mL
¼ cup	dry white wine	50 mL
8 oz	cooked lobster meat, minced	240 g
½ tsp	salt	2 mL
¼ tsp	white pepper	1 mL
¼ tsp	paprika	1 mL

In a medium-sized soup pot over medium heat, melt butter. Add onion and celery, and sauté for 5 minutes or until onions are transparent. Sprinkle with flour, and cook an additional 3 minutes, stirring constantly. Slowly add milk or cream, chicken stock and wine, whisking constantly until mixture is smooth and begins to thicken. Add minced lobster meat and any juices,* salt, pepper and paprika and simmer for 15 minutes over low heat, stirring occasionally. Remove from heat and purée in a blender. Serve hot with minced chives.

If using frozen canned lobster, thaw and include the juices. If using fresh cooked lobster, reserve the lobster liquor when shelling the lobster and add to the bisque.

Makes 4 servings.

LIGHTHOUSE LOBSTER PASTA

Nova Scotia lobster is the most important species in the province's multi-million-dollar seafood industry.

Cold lobster and pasta tossed with a creamy light dressing makes a great summer lunch or light one-dish supper meal.

½ cup	olive oil	125 mL
½ cup	sour cream	125 mL
¼ cup	lemon juice	50 mL
½ cup	chopped fresh dill	125 mL
1	clove garlic, crushed	1
2 cups	lobster meat, cooked and chopped or 1 tin (11.3 oz/312 mL) frozen lobster meat	500 mL
1 cup	chopped ripe tomato	250 mL
2 tbsp	finely chopped green onion	25 mL
1 tsp	freshly ground black pepper	5 mL
8 oz	dry fusilli pasta	250 g

In a medium-sized bowl, combine olive oil, sour cream, lemon juice, dill and garlic. Whisk until well blended. Add lobster meat, chopped tomato, green onion and pepper. Toss until well mixed. Cover and refrigerate for 1 hour to blend flavors.

Cook pasta in salted boiling water until tender (8 to 10 minutes). Drain the pasta and rinse with cold water to stop the cooking process. Drain and cool.

Add pasta to lobster mixture. Toss well. Cover and refrigerate for at least 1 hour before serving.

Makes 4 servings.

LOBSTER ROLL

The ultimate Nova Scotia "fast food" lends itself to picnics on the beach or lunch for two on the deck. For a lighter variation, use pita pockets instead of the traditional roll.

When draining canned frozen lobster for this or other recipes, save and freeze the liquid to add to your favorite seafood chowder for extra flavor.

1	11.3 oz (312 mL) can frozen lobster meat*		1
⅓–¾ cup	mayonnaise	125 mL	175 mL
2 tsp	lemon juice		10 mL
3 tbsp	diced celery		45 mL
2 tbsp	minced onion (optional)		25 mL

Thaw and drain lobster meat. Chop into bite-sized pieces. In a small mixing bowl, combine mayonnaise with lemon juice, celery and onion. Add to lobster and mix well.

Spread the lobster salad on your favorite bread, croissant or use as a pita bread filling.

*Yields approximately 2 cups (500 mL) of lobster meat.

Makes 4 to 6 servings.

SEAFOOD PIE

*Served cold, this dish is a great traveler and is sure
to be a hit at a picnic or any other social event.
Use crab, shrimp, lobster or a combination of
the three. The pie is also delicious when served
warm from the oven with a side salad.*

¼ cup	grated Parmesan cheese	50 mL
½ cup	sliced mushrooms	125 mL
½ cup	chopped green onions	125 mL
⅔ cup	cooked crab meat	150 mL
⅔ cup	cooked lobster meat	150 mL
1 cup	cooked shrimp	250 mL
2	large eggs	2
⅔ cup	milk	150 mL
¼ cup	dry white wine	50 mL
¼ cup	fresh chopped parsley	50 mL
¼ tsp	salt	1 mL
¼ tsp	freshly ground black pepper	1 mL
¼ tsp	ground nutmeg	1 mL
	Pastry for a double pie crust (recipe on page 7)	

Line a 9-inch (23-cm) deep-dish pie plate with the pastry. Sprinkle half of the Parmesan cheese over the bottom. Layer the mushrooms, green onions and seafood until they are all used. In a food processor, combine the remaining cheese, eggs, milk, wine, parsley and seasoning. Process until smooth. Pour the milk mixture over the seafood mixture until seafood is just covered, taking care not to overfill. Cover with top pie crust. Trim and seal the edges, and cut slits in the top for the steam to escape.

Bake in a preheated 400°F (200°C) oven for 15 minutes, then reduce the heat to 350°F (180°C) and cook for an additional 30 minutes or until a tester inserted in the center comes out clean. Cool on a metal rack.

Makes 8 servings.

PIE CRUST FOR ONE DOUBLE-CRUST PIE

3 cups	flour	750 mL
1 tsp	salt	5 mL
½ cup	cold shortening, cubed	125 mL
½ cup	cold butter or margarine, cubed	125 mL
1	egg	1
2 tsp	white vinegar	10 mL
	Ice cold water	

Combine flour and salt in a large mixing bowl. Cut in cubed butter or margarine and shortening using a pastry blender or two knives until mixture resembles fine crumbs with some larger pieces. In a liquid measuring cup, beat the egg until foamy and add vinegar and enough ice water to make ⅔ cup (150 mL). Gradually sprinkle over the flour mixture, tossing with a fork just until dough holds together. Divide into two equal balls, and flatten slightly with your hands. Wrap and refrigerate for 30 minutes. (Dough may be kept refrigerated for up to 3 days or frozen for up to 3 months.) Remove pastry from refrigerator 15 minutes before rolling it out.

Food processor method: Into a food processor fitted with a metal blade, measure the flour and salt. With an on/off motion, cut in the butter or margarine and the shortening until mixture resembles fine crumbs, with some larger pieces. Combine liquids as with the conventional method. With the motor running, add the egg mixture all at once. Process just until dough begins to clump together—do not let it form into a ball. Remove from processor, and form into two balls. Wrap and refrigerate for 30 minutes, removing 15 minutes before rolling out.

Makes one 9- or 10-inch (23- or 25-cm)
double pie crust.

NEVER FAIL PIE CRUST

5¼ cups	all-purpose flour	1.3 L
1½ tsp	salt	7 mL
1 lb	lard or shortening	454 g
1	egg	1
1 tbsp	white vinegar	15 mL
	Ice cold water	

In a large bowl, combine the flour with the salt. Using a pastry blender or two knives, cut in lard or shortening until mixture resembles fine crumbs with a few larger pieces. In a measuring cup, beat together egg and vinegar until blended. Add enough ice water to make 1 cup (250 mL). Stir well. Gradually add just enough egg mixture, 1 tbsp (15 mL) at a time, to flour mixture, to make dough hold together. Divide dough into 6 portions and shape each into a ball. Wrap in plastic wrap, and refrigerate for 30 minutes. At this point, dough may be refrigerated for up to 1 week, or placed in the freezer for up to 3 months. Remove pastry from refrigerator 15 minutes before rolling it out.

*Makes enough for three 9-inch (23-cm)
double-crust pies.*

SEAFOOD STEW

Combining shellfish and white fish is a European tradition—bouillabaisse is one famous example. Here we use shrimp and leave the choice of the white fish up to you. Zucchini, tomato and green pepper tie this stew to its zesty Mediterranean roots.

White fish fillets can be any of the following or a combination thereof: cusk, haddock, halibut, hake, ocean catfish, ocean perch, cod, monkfish, blue shark, Boston bluefish or turbot.

1 lb	white fish fillets	500 g
½ lb	cooked shrimp	250 g
2 tbsp	vegetable oil	25 mL
2	cloves garlic, minced	2
1	medium onion, coarsely diced	1
12	large mushrooms, quartered	12
1	green pepper, coarsely diced	1
3	medium carrots, thinly sliced	3
2	small zucchini, sliced	2
3 cups	fresh tomatoes, chopped, or 28 oz (796 mL) canned	750 mL
½ tsp	dried thyme	2 mL
1 tsp	dried basil	5 mL
¼ tsp	crushed chilies	1 mL

Remove any bones from fish fillet and cut flesh into bite-sized pieces. If using frozen shrimp, thaw. In a large saucepan, heat the oil over medium heat and sauté the garlic, onion, mushrooms and green pepper for 5 minutes. Add carrots, zucchini, tomatoes and seasoning. Bring to a boil, then reduce heat and simmer for 15 minutes, stirring occasionally. Add white fish and cook uncovered for 5 minutes. Add shrimp and heat for 2 minutes. Adjust seasonings with salt and pepper to taste. Serve hot.

Makes 4 to 6 servings.

HARVEST LOBSTER SALAD

A 1-lb (500-g) lobster contains approximately ¼ lb (125 g) or ⅔ cup (150 mL) of meat.

Corn and zucchini add a surprising crunch to this salad, which makes a tasty first course or buffet selection. Use fresh corn if it's available—it takes no time at all to cut the kernels off the cob, and the taste difference is dramatic.

1	medium-sized zucchini	1
½ cup	corn kernels, fresh from a cob or frozen	125 mL
2 cups	lobster meat or 1 can (11.3 oz/ 312 mL) frozen lobster	500 mL
¼ cup	mayonnaise	50 mL
1 tbsp	lemon juice	15 mL
	Salt and pepper to taste	
6	basil leaves, washed and finely chopped	6

Trim the ends of the zucchini and cut into ¼-inch (6-mm) slices. Cut each slice in half to make a half-moon shape. Blanch the zucchini and corn for 1 minute in a saucepan of boiling water over medium high heat. Drain and allow to cool in a medium-sized bowl.

Cut the lobster meat (thawed and drained if using frozen) into ½-inch (1-cm) pieces and add to the bowl of cooled vegetables.

In a small bowl, combine the mayonnaise, lemon juice and salt and pepper to taste, and stir until well blended. Add dressing to the lobster and vegetable mixture, and toss to coat well. Add chopped basil and toss gently again. To serve, mound the salad on a bed of lettuce on a salad plate, and garnish with a whole basil leaf and a lemon wedge.

Makes 6 servings.

Hot Lobster

Our neighbors in Maine call this dish "lobster fried over cold." It is a perfect example of how simple cooking and ingredients can magically produce the most delicious results.

2 cups	cooked lobster meat	500 mL
¼ cup	butter	50 mL
¼ cup	heavy or whipping cream (35%)	50 mL

Cut the lobster into bite-sized pieces. In a heavy-bottomed skillet, melt the butter, add the lobster and sauté until the lobster is hot, approximately 10 minutes. Gradually add cream, stirring to combine. Serve at once on toast or with a hot biscuit.

Makes 4 servings.

How to cook a lobster

Lobster is at its best when prepared as simply as possible and served either hot or cold, shelled or in the shell, and accompanied by melted butter, lemon wedges and lots of napkins. The traditional Nova Scotia way of cooking lobster is in a boiling pot of salt water directly from the ocean on a sandy beach over an open fire.

To prepare lobster, first ensure that it is alive by checking for movement—pull its tail back to see if it springs back to the curled position. Put the live lobster head-first into salted boiling water; use 1 tbsp (15 mL) salt per 1 quart (1 L) water. Cover the pot. Begin timing once the water returns to a rolling boil. Cook for 10 minutes for the first 1 lb (500 g) and 3 minutes for each additional 1 lb (500 g). The lobster is cooked when it is bright red and the legs pull away from the body with ease.

LOBSTER CANAPÉS

The safest way to thaw frozen canned lobster meat is to place the unopened can in cold water in the refrigerator. Allow 2 hours per pound (500 g) for thawing. Do not thaw in warm water or at room temperature.

Wow your guests with this easy-to-make lobster purée, which can be used as a spread or piped on crackers for delicious canapés.

2 cups	cooked lobster meat or 1 can frozen (11.3 oz/312 mL)	500 mL
1	large package (250 g) softened cream cheese	1
1 tbsp	lemon juice	15 mL
2 tbsp	seafood sauce	25 mL
2 tbsp	chopped fresh dill or parsley Salt and pepper to taste	25 mL

If using frozen lobster, thaw and drain, removing any cartilage. Put lobster in a food processor and process until pieces are broken up. Add cream cheese, lemon juice, seafood sauce, dill, salt and pepper, and process until smooth. Adjust seasonings and chill until serving time.

To serve, either pipe with a piping bag or spread onto crackers or toast points. Garnish with fresh dill or parsley. For an added taste sensation, put a small piece of lobster on top of the spread. Or, into small purchased canapé cups, put a small piece of lobster and top with the spread to make a miniature hidden treasure.

FRUITS DE MER

*The medley of scallops, shrimp and lobster starts
with a quick sauté in a fragrant garlic-scented olive oil.
Easy-to-prepare béchamel coats the fish with
a rich, smooth sauce.*

3 tbsp	olive oil	45 mL
2	cloves garlic, chopped	2
½ tsp	cumin	2 mL
½ tsp	salt	2 mL
1 tsp	black peppercorns, cracked	5 mL
¾ lb	scallops	360 g
2 cups	shrimp	500 mL
2 cups	béchamel sauce	500 mL
	(recipe page 14)	
½ lb	cooked lobster meat	250 g
1	pkg. dry fusilli pasta (375 g)	1

*Although Nova
Scotia is not widely
known for its
shrimp, our cold-
water Northern
pink shrimp makes
up for its lack of
size with its sweet
delicate flavor. Our
shrimp are greatly
appreciated in
Europe and Japan,
where shrimp feasts
are celebrated with
mounds of shrimp
arrayed on a table.
The guests peel them
and dip them in
sauce.*

In a medium saucepan, heat the olive oil over low heat, then sauté
the garlic, cumin, salt and pepper in it for 30 seconds. Increase the
heat to medium high and add the scallops and shrimp. Sauté an
additional 2 minutes. Add the béchamel sauce and simmer for 2
minutes. Add lobster and simmer an additional 1 minute.

Cook pasta as directed on package. Divide the pasta on four
warmed plates and spoon seafood mixture on top. Garnish with
fresh parsley and lemon slice.

Makes 4 to 6 servings.

Béchamel Sauce

¼ cup	butter	50 mL
¼ cup	all-purpose flour	50 mL
2 cups	milk	500 mL
1 tsp	lemon juice	5 mL
1 tsp	salt	5 mL
	Dash of black pepper	
	Dash of ground nutmeg	

In a small saucepan, melt the butter, and blend in the flour until smooth. Cook for 2 minutes, stirring constantly. Add milk, lemon juice, salt, pepper and nutmeg, whisking constantly until the sauce is smooth and thick.

Makes 2 cups (500 mL).

KING OF THE SEA SALAD

Sweet, chewy lobster and silky scallops combine well in this elegant salad. The sugar and vinegar give a piquant tang that complements the seafood.

2	cloves garlic, minced	2
2 tbsp	olive oil	25 mL
½ lb	scallops	250 g
½ lb	cooked lobster meat	250 g
½ cup	tomatoes, seeded and finely chopped	125 mL
1	small red onion, thinly sliced	1
2 tbsp	olive oil	25 mL
2 tbsp	white vinegar	25 mL
1 tsp	paprika	5 mL
1 tsp	granulated sugar	5 mL
	Salt and pepper to taste	

In a skillet, over medium heat, sauté the garlic in the olive oil for 1 minute. Add the scallops and sauté for 2 minutes. Stir in lobster, tomatoes and red onion. Remove from heat, transfer to a mixing bowl and allow to cool. In a small bowl, whisk together olive oil, vinegar, paprika and sugar until well blended, then add salt and pepper to taste.

Gently toss the lobster and scallops with the dressing until well coated. To serve, place on a bed of mixed greens garnished with a lemon slice and fresh dill.

Makes 4 servings.

NOVA SCOTIA CRAB CAKES

The Atlantic snow crab (also known as spider or queen crab) has four pairs of long thin legs, a pair of claws and a reddish shell. Its meat is lean, mild and delicately sweet.

The key to delicate crab cakes is to use lots of crab meat relative to the other ingredients.

1	egg	1
1 tbsp	dry mustard	15 mL
2 tsp	lemon juice	10 mL
2 tsp	red wine vinegar	10 mL
½ cup	vegetable oil	125 mL
¼ cup	olive oil	50 mL
1 lb	cooked crab meat	500 g
2 tbsp	chopped fresh parsley	25 mL
¼ cup	finely chopped green pepper	50 mL
¼ cup	finely chopped red pepper	50 mL
¼ cup	finely chopped onion	50 mL
4 cups	fresh, soft bread crumbs	1 L

In a food processor, blend the egg, dry mustard, lemon juice and vinegar until smooth. With the processor running, gradually add the vegetable and olive oils to the egg mixture to form a smooth dressing. In a mixing bowl, combine the dressing mixture with the crab meat, along with the parsley, green and red peppers and onion, stirring to blend well. Blend in 2 cups (500 mL) of the bread crumbs. Shape crab mixture into patties by first forming into 3-inch (8-cm) balls, roll them in remaining bread crumbs and then flatten them out with your hands.

Fry them in a small amount of butter over medium heat until golden brown on both sides.

Makes 4 servings.

CRAB DIP

Here is an easy-to-make hors d'oeuvre or light snack that can be spread on a variety of crackers or breads. One such bread is pita, which makes a tasty crisp treat when made into chips. To make pita chips, cut the bread in small triangles. Brush lightly with some vegetable oil and sprinkle with salt and pepper. Bake in a preheated 375°F (190°C) oven for 15 minutes.

2 cups	cooked crab meat (1 can 11.3 oz/312 mL)	500 mL
1	large package (250 g) cream cheese, softened	1
2 tbsp	seafood or chili sauce	25 mL
⅓ cup	creamy dressing*	75 mL
½ tsp	prepared mustard	2 mL
1 tbsp	grated onion	15 mL
1 tbsp	chopped fresh parsley	15 mL
¼ cup	crushed cracker crumbs	50 mL
2 tbsp	butter	25 mL

In a food processor, process crab meat until pieces are broken up. Add cream cheese, seafood sauce, mayonnaise, mustard, grated onion and parsley and process until ingredients are well blended.

Put crab mixture in a 4-cup (1-L) casserole dish and top with cracker crumbs. Dot with butter. Bake in a preheated 350°F (180°C) oven for 15 minutes. Serve hot.

*Homemade creamy dressing adds extra tang to this recipe and many of the other recipes contained in this book. The following microwave version makes homemade creamy dressing a quick alternative to store-bought.

CREAMY DRESSING

2 tbsp	all-purpose flour	25 mL
1 tsp	salt	5 mL
1 tsp	dry mustard	5 mL
⅔ cup	granulated sugar	150 mL
1	egg	1
¾ cup	white vinegar	175 mL
¾ cup	milk	175 mL

In a microwave-safe bowl, blend flour, salt, mustard and sugar. Add egg, vinegar and milk and whisk until well blended and smooth. Microwave for 5 minutes on high power. Stir or whisk at the 2½-minute mark to blend. Remove from microwave, stir and cool before using.

This recipe can also be made in a double boiler on top of the stove. Follow mixing procedure and cook until mixture thickens to mayonnaise consistency, stirring occasionally to prevent sticking.

Makes 2 cups (500 mL).

CHAPTER TWO

SHELLFISH

Scallops, oysters, clams and mussels are the shellfish harvested both on and off the shores of Nova Scotia. These seafood varieties are incredibly versatile and serve as the main ingredient in a vast array of chowders, salads and entrées. It is important to purchase your shellfish from a market you trust. Properly harvested, stored and handled, these bivalves offer great eating. Be demanding, and insist on the freshest product. Nova Scotia fishermen harvest great quantities of scallops and mussels for both domestic use and export. Oysters and clams are not as widely fished and are mainly used in our own kitchens and neighborhood restaurants. Of course, all of our recipes use locally collected shellfish, and the quicker a bivalve goes from the sea to the table, the more wonderful the result.

Scallops are perhaps the most beautiful of the harvested shellfish. The shell that houses the snowy white muscle that we eat is often recycled for use as a small plate or dish. The scallop is perhaps the most versatile shellfish as well. Jasper White, the famous New England chef, suggests that scallops can be eaten "raw, cured, smoked, fried, stir fried, sautéed, grilled, broiled, poached or steamed." They are rich and nutritious, and small portions are satisfying. The key to success in preparing the scallop is to avoid overcooking, which produces a tough, rubbery result.

The mussel is a shellfish that is only recently becoming a staple in the home kitchen, although it has long been an integral part of the clambake or beach barbecue. Mussels are easily found at the shore, and collecting them and roasting them in the coals of the beach bonfire, or tossing them into a pot to steam open, is a satisfying way to spend time at the shore. Now that marvelous mussels are cultivated by the fast-growing aquaculture business, fresh mussels can easily be found in the markets.

Kaija Lind is in the forefront of this industry. From a base in the old village of Ship Harbour on the sparsely populated eastern shore of Nova Scotia, her business, Aqua Nova Mussel Farm, raises the blue mussel variety most often found in the provincial waters. Kaija studied marine biology at Halifax's Dalhousie University, home of one of the finest such departments in the world. She fascinated us with the description of the business. A mussel farmer uses very natural techniques to grow his or her crop of cultivated mussels, which are plump, clean and very tasty. In the late spring, as the water warms a bit, the cultivated and wild mussels release their "seed"; these float freely for a couple of weeks, eventually anchoring themselves on the rope or plastic mesh placed in the water by the farmer. Over the summer, the mussels will grow to something under an inch (2.5 cm), at which time they are collected and sorted by size. They are then returned to the water in hollow tubes, each holding mussels of similar size, and are left to grow for another year or year and a half. The tubes, which are from 8 to 18 feet (2 to 5 m) in length and sunk well below the surface of the ocean to protect the mussels from winter ice and turbulent weather, have holes through which the mussel grows and attaches itself to the rope. With such coddling, the shell that develops is thinner than that of the wild mussel, which needs heavier armor to fend off the elements. The cultivated mussel is also bigger than its wild cousin. The mussel is delivered to the distributor within several hours of harvesting. Like the oyster, a mussel that ingests a bit of sand or other irritant will develop a small pearl. Would-be gem collectors are advised to seek out the wild mussel, since farming techniques reduce the irritants in the water.

The cultivated mussel needs little cleaning. A quick tug will remove any remnant of the rope the shellfish clung to in the water, and a brief rinse is all that is needed. Steam with some white wine and garlic, or place on the grill for a few minutes. Discard any mussel whose shell does not open after cooking. The meat can be removed from the shell for use in other dishes, or eaten right from the shell and dipped in some lemon butter. Mussels, like lobster, are enjoyed more when dining formalities are set aside and your hands become your primary utensil.

BUBBLY BAKE

Serve hot and bubbly right from the oven.
Rice and steamed asparagus are good side dishes to
round out the meal.

1 lb	scallops	500 g
¼ cup	butter or margarine	50 mL
2 tbsp	finely chopped green onions	25 mL
½ cup	sliced mushrooms	125 mL
2 tbsp	all-purpose flour	25 mL
⅓ cup	18% cream	75 mL
⅓ cup	white wine	75 mL
1 tsp	salt	5 mL
	Fresh ground black pepper to taste	
½ cup	bread crumbs	125 mL

Rinse scallops and set aside. In a saucepan, melt butter. Sauté green onions and mushrooms until onions become transparent. Add flour and mix thoroughly; add cream and stir until sauce has slightly thickened. Add wine, salt and pepper, stirring until completely blended. Add scallops and pour into a 1½-quart (1.5-L) casserole dish. Top with bread crumbs. Bake in a preheated 350°F (180°C) oven for 25 minutes.

Makes 4 servings.

Each summer the larger ferries travel between Portland and Bar Harbor in Maine and Saint John in New Brunswick, to Yarmouth and Digby, Nova Scotia. As they arrive in port, those on deck may see a jumble of scallop boats representing a major part of the Western Nova Scotia economy. There are two major classifications of scallops: bay scallops and sea scallops. The famous Digby scallop is the sea variety.

CATCH 57

The origin of this unusual name is unknown. The rich Hollandaise sauce that tops this combination of shellfish and whitefish makes for a special dish. Serve with rice or noodles and your favorite vegetable.

6 oz	haddock fillet	180 g
2 oz	scallops	60 g
⅓ cup	shrimp	75 mL
⅓ cup	Hollandaise sauce	75 mL
	(see recipe below)	

Put haddock in a lightly buttered baking dish. Top with scallops and shrimp. Bake in a preheated 350°F (180°C) oven for 8 to 10 minutes or until haddock flakes easily. Remove from oven and top with Hollandaise sauce. Return to oven for 1 or 2 minutes.

Makes 2 servings.

Hollandaise Sauce

3	egg yolks, lightly beaten	3
2 tbsp	lemon juice	25 mL
⅔ cup	butter	150 mL
	Salt	
	Pinch of cayenne pepper (optional)	

Put egg yolks in the top of a double boiler over hot but not boiling water. Whisk in 1 tbsp (15 mL) lemon juice and 1 tbsp (15 mL) of butter until the butter is melted. Whisk in the remaining butter about 2 tbsp (25 mL) at a time until it is all melted and the sauce begins to thicken. Add the remaining lemon juice, salt and cayenne pepper to taste. Continue heating until the sauce is thick and smooth. Keep sauce warm but do not overcook.

Scallop Chowder

Most chowders are similar in style, with seafood, cream or milk and potatoes predominating. But different seafood—clams, mussels or, as in this recipe, scallops—makes each chowder distinct. Scallop chowder is rich enough to serve as a one-dish meal, especially if accompanied by fresh biscuits or bread.

All scallops are best cooked briefly. Overcooking toughens the muscle and affects the flavor.

1 lb	scallops	500 g
2 tbsp	butter	25 mL
1	onion, chopped	1
½ cup	chopped celery	125 mL
2 cups	diced raw potatoes	500 mL
½ cup	sliced carrots	125 mL
2 cups	boiling water	500 mL
1 tsp	salt	5 mL
1 tsp	thyme	5 mL
dash	pepper	dash
1½ cups	whole milk	375 mL
¾ cup	light cream (18%)	175 mL
	Paprika	

Scallops can be cut in half if desired. In a heavy saucepan over medium heat, melt butter. Add onion, celery and sauté until tender. Add potatoes, carrots, water, salt, thyme and pepper. Cover and simmer for 10 to 15 minutes or until vegetables are tender. Add the scallops and simmer for 8 to 10 minutes or until flesh becomes opaque. Add the milk and cream, heat gently. Do not boil. Sprinkle each serving with paprika.

Makes 6 servings.

HONEY GRILLED SCALLOPS

Asian culinary influences are showing up in Nova Scotia thanks to recent Chinese and Vietnamese immigrants. Lime, ginger and sesame are great complementary flavors for the briny scallop. Honey creates a golden glaze whether you're cooking over hot coals or under a broiler.

3 tbsp	freshly squeezed lime juice	45 mL
1 tsp	sesame oil	5 mL
2 tsp	vegetable oil	10 mL
1 tbsp	liquid honey	15 mL
1 tbsp	soy sauce	15 mL
2 tsp	grated fresh ginger	10 mL
1 lb	scallops	500 g
2 tbsp	sesame seeds (optional)	25 mL

In a small bowl, whisk together lime juice, sesame oil, vegetable oil, honey, soy sauce and ginger. Put scallops in a large freezer bag and pour marinade over them. Seal tightly and refrigerate for 1 hour, turning the bag after 30 minutes. Remove the scallops, reserving the marinade. Thread four scallops on each skewer. (If using wooden skewers, soak them in water for 1 hour prior to grilling). Brush scallops with some of the marinade. Place skewers on broiler pan or a well-oiled rack or basket, placed 4 to 6 inches (10 to 15 cm) from the heat source. Grill or broil for 2 to 3 minutes, turn, brush with marinade and cook an additional 2 minutes. Remove from heat and roll in sesame seeds on a flat plate until each scallop is well coated.

Makes 4 servings.

Sautéed Digby Scallops with Honey Onion Chutney

The sweet flavors of three different ingredients—honey, onions and scallops—blend to create a distinctive and delicious entrée. This chutney is also nice with a grilled white fish, such as haddock.

Chutney

1 tbsp	butter	15 mL
1	whole onion, thinly sliced	1
¼ cup	white vinegar	50 mL
¾ cup	liquid honey	175 mL
1 tsp	paprika	5 mL

In a small saucepan, melt butter and sauté onion until golden. Add vinegar to onion, and stir to combine. Add honey and paprika, stirring well. Continue cooking chutney over medium heat until it begins to thicken.

Scallops

1 tbsp	butter	15 mL
1 tsp	lemon juice	5 mL
1 lb	Digby scallops	500 g

In a skillet over medium heat, melt butter. Add lemon juice and scallops and lightly sauté until fork tender. Put scallops on warmed serving plates and top with chutney.

Makes 4 servings.

MARINATED MUSSELS

Given their great taste and very economical price, mussels are still an underused shellfish in most of North America, although, like the Europeans, we Nova Scotians are very fond of them. The cultivated mussel is cleaner than the wild variety. Remove the "beard" that connects the bivalve to the rock or rope that it has called home. Mussels can be kept for two or three days, not in water, which will kill them, but wrapped in damp newspaper.

A terrific dish to serve at a party, for a buffet or as an appetizer. The red wine, balsamic vinegar and garlic infuse the mussels with a punchy flavor.

¾ cup	red wine	175 mL
1	clove garlic, chopped	1
1	bay leaf	1
½ cup	chopped onions	125 mL
4 to 5 lbs	mussels	2 kg

Put red wine, garlic, bay leaf and onions in a deep saucepan and bring to a boil. Add mussels and cover. Let mussels steam for 3 to 5 minutes, or until they are opened. Remove mussels, discarding any that do not open, and transfer mussels in their shell to a large serving bowl.

Dice the following vegetables, put in a bowl. Set aside.

½	small green pepper	½
½	small red pepper	½
½	small yellow pepper	½
½	small red onion	½

Marinade

1 cup	olive oil	250 mL
½ cup	balsamic vinegar	125 mL
1	garlic clove, minced	1
	Salt and pepper to taste	

Measure the above ingredients into an air-tight container or a Ziplock bag and shake well. Turn occasionally for even marinating. Add the reserved diced vegetables and stir to coat. Pour the mixture over the reserved mussels. Refrigerate until 15 minutes before serving.

Make 6 servings.

MUSSEL CHOWDER

We prepare this chowder in a style similar to clam chowder but the mussels give a more pronounced "briny" flavor. Serve piping hot with crusty bread.

4 to 5 lbs	mussels	2 kg
½ cup	water or white wine	125 mL
1 tbsp	butter	15 mL
¾ cup	diced onions	175 mL
2 tbsp	flour	25 mL
2 cups	diced potatoes	500 mL
4 cups	milk	1 L
2 cups	light cream (18%)	500 mL
	Salt and pepper to taste	
4	bacon strips, fried crisp	4

Scrub mussels, trim beard or byssus threads, and steam open, 3 to 5 minutes in ½ cup (125 mL) water or white wine. Remove meats, strain and reserve broth. Add enough hot water to broth to make 4 cups (1 L).

Melt butter in a medium saucepan. Add onions and sauté until transparent. Add flour and stir to blend thoroughly. Gradually add the broth and water mixture, stirring well, and bring to a boil. Add the potatoes and simmer until they are tender, about 15 minutes. Add mussels and gently stir in milk and cream to heat, but do not boil. Season lightly with salt and pepper. Garnish with crumbled bacon strips.

Makes 6 servings.

MUSSELS WITH GARLIC SAUCE

Cultivated mussels will often gape open. When tapped or rinsed under cold water, they should close. Discard any that do not close.

Farm-raised mussels are abundantly available and appear regularly at the markets and on restaurant menus everywhere. This dish can be made in 20 minutes or less.

2 lbs	mussels	1 kg
2 tbsp	butter	25 mL
2	green onions, chopped	2
2	cloves garlic, minced	2
12	whole black peppercorns	12
¾ cup	dry white wine	175 mL
	Juice of half a lemon	
1 tbsp	chopped fresh thyme	15 mL
	or ¼ tsp (1 mL) dried	
½ tsp	salt	2 mL

Scrub the mussels under cold running water, removing the beard or byssus.

In a large stock pot or wok, melt butter and add green onions, garlic, peppercorns, wine, lemon juice, thyme and salt. Bring to a boil. Add the mussels and cook covered, for 6 to 8 minutes over high heat until mussels open. Remove from heat and remove mussels with a slotted spoon into serving bowls. Discard any unopened mussels.

Strain cooking broth through a fine sieve into a bowl and pour over cooked mussels. Top with a few grinds of fresh black pepper and serve with a good crusty bread to soak up the broth.

Makes 4 servings.

Tomato Basil Mussels

Mussels swimming in a deep red, fragrant sauce make for a quickly emptied plate. Once you've eaten the mussels, don't resist the urge to use some crusty bread to sop up the sauce in the bowl.

2 lbs	mussels	1 kg
2 tbsp	olive oil	25 mL
¼ cup	sliced green onions	50 mL
1	clove garlic, minced	1
1	19-oz (540-mL) can tomatoes, drained and chopped	1
½ cup	dry white wine or chicken stock	125 mL
1 tsp	dried basil	5 mL
¼ tsp	Tabasco sauce	1 mL
1 tsp	balsamic vinegar	5 mL
	Salt and pepper to taste	

Barbecue mussels by placing them on a grill 4 inches (10 cm) from the hot coals. Barbecue for 5 to 15 minutes or until the shells open. Serve with melted butter.

Rinse mussels in cold water, and remove byssus threads. Discard any mussels that do not close.

Heat oil in a large saucepan. Add 2 tbsp (25 mL) of the onions and the garlic. Sauté until softened, 1 to 2 minutes. Add the tomatoes, wine (or chicken stock), basil and Tabasco sauce and bring to a boil. Add the mussels. Cover and steam until mussels open, 3 to 5 minutes. Discard any mussels that do not open.

Transfer the mussels to a serving bowl. Stir vinegar into the tomato mixture and season with salt and pepper to taste. Pour over the mussels and sprinkle with the remaining onion.

Makes 2 main course or 4 appetizer servings.

CREAM OF ASPARAGUS AND OYSTER SOUP

While not as well known or abundant as its Prince Edward Island cousin, the Malpeque, Nova Scotians enjoy local Atlantic oysters. Fresh oysters are best enjoyed between September and June. They spawn in the warmer months and develop a less-desirable soft texture. As with all shellfish there should be no "fishy" or acidic odor about them, and the liquid, or "liquor," should be clear.

Of all the shellfish, oysters have the most intense flavor of the sea and, in this recipe, they add a nice crunch as well. The soup's creaminess comes from the smooth texture of puréed asparagus.

2 lbs	asparagus	1 kg
1 tbsp	butter	15 mL
1	clove garlic, minced	1
1	medium onion, diced	1
1	celery stalk, diced	1
2 cups	chicken stock	500 mL
1	bouquet garni (thyme, bay leaf, parsley tied in cheesecloth)	1
3 drops	Tabasco sauce	3 drops
	Salt and pepper	
1	medium potato, diced	1
½ cup	heavy or whipping cream (35%)	125 mL
	Dash of nutmeg	
12	oysters, shucked, cut in half and with their liquor reserved	12
1 tbsp	chopped chives or parsley	15 mL

Trim the tough ends from the asparagus and cut the spears 1 inch (2.5 cm) from the tip. Cook the tips and reserve for garnish. Coarsely chop the remaining asparagus stalks. In a saucepan, melt the butter and add the asparagus pieces, garlic, onion and celery. Cook until vegetables appear shiny, about 5 minutes. Add the chicken stock, bouquet garni, Tabasco sauce and a good pinch of salt and pepper. Let this simmer for 10 minutes and then add the potato; add a bit more water if necessary, just to cover vegetables. Cook an additional 20 minutes and then add the cream and nutmeg. Bring to a boil and remove from heat. Remove bouquet garni. Put mixture in a blender or processor and process just until mixture appears thickened. Strain through a medium sieve and adjust the seasonings.

To serve, add the oysters raw, with their liquor, or bring to a gentle boil just to heat. Garnish the soup with the reserved spears of asparagus and a sprinkle of chives or parsley.

Makes 4 to 6 servings.

OYSTER ROAST

A staple of the clambake on the beach, these oysters work equally well on the grill. A perfect dish for those who don't like shucking oysters, since the shell opens on its own. You can use clams instead of oysters, if you like.

| 36 | oysters | 36 |
| | Melted butter | |

Scrub oysters' shells thoroughly. Place oysters on the grill or broiler about 4 inches (10 cm) from heat source. Roast for 15 minutes or until shells begin to open. Remove from heat and serve in their shells with melted butter.

Makes 6 servings.

Bouquet garni is a mixture of herbs and spices tied in a cheesecloth bag. Toss it in stews, sauces or soups and discard it at the end of the cooking process. Typical ingredients of a bouquet garni are celery, bay leaf, thyme and green onion.

OYSTER STEW

Nova Scotia is gaining a reputation for its native or Atlantic oysters with their distinctive, salty taste.

Whole oysters frozen with their liquor can be purchased in most markets. They work well in this stew if you don't have the time or inclination to shuck the fresh ones, and it cuts the preparation time to 30 minutes or so.

¼ cup	butter	50 mL
1 cup	chopped celery	250 mL
2	medium onions, finely chopped	2
	(or 1 onion and 1 cup [250 mL] chopped leeks)	
1 cup	finely grated carrots (optional)	250 mL
¼ cup	butter	50 mL
⅓ cup	flour	75 mL
2 cups	milk (whole or 2%)	500 mL
2 cups	cream (10%)	500 mL
2 cups	oysters (about 30), shucked	500 mL
	with their liquor	
	Salt and pepper to taste	

In a large saucepan, heat ¼ cup (50 mL) butter and stir in vegetables; cover tightly and cook over low heat for 10 to 15 minutes, until vegetables are tender. Stir occasionally and do not allow to brown.

To make white sauce, use medium-sized saucepan to melt remaining ¼ cup (50 mL) butter. Add flour, stir to form a paste and cook for 1 to 2 minutes. Do not brown. Remove from heat and gradually beat in milk. Return to heat and cook until sauce is thickened; beat until smooth. Gradually add light cream, beating constantly. Stir sauce into vegetable mixture.

In another saucepan, over low heat, cook oysters in their liquor, uncovered, for 3 to 5 minutes or until oysters just start to curl. Do not boil. Stir oysters and liquor into vegetable mixture and heat through slowly.

Season with salt and pepper to taste and pour into heated serving bowls.

Makes 6 servings.

CLAM STUFFED MUSHROOM CAPS

Mushrooms lend themselves to being stuffed with a variety of fillings. Our version uses sweet clam meat combined with crunchy peppers and a sprinkle of tangy Parmesan cheese.

1½ cups	cooked clams*	375 mL
⅓ cup	butter	75 mL
⅓ cup	finely diced green pepper	75 mL
⅓ cup	finely diced red pepper	75 mL
3 tbsp	finely chopped onion	45 mL
3 tbsp	dry white wine	45 mL
1 cup	finely chopped white bread crumbs	250 mL
	Salt and pepper to taste	
20	large mushroom caps	20
⅓ cup	grated Parmesan cheese	75 mL

* To cook fresh clams, put them into a large pot with about 1 inch (2.5 cm) of water. Cover the pot and bring the water to a boil; the clams should steam open in about 5 minutes. Cook just until the shells have opened— overcooking will make them tough. Discard any clams that do not open.

Dice the clam meat. Melt the butter in a skillet and sauté clam meat, green and red peppers and onions until onions are transparent. Add the white wine and simmer until the clams are tender. Add bread crumbs and seasonings, and mix until well combined.

Wash mushrooms and remove stems. Spoon clam stuffing into inverted mushroom caps and sprinkle with Parmesan cheese. Bake in a preheated 350°F (180°C) oven for 5 minutes or until golden brown.

Makes 4 appetizer servings.

CLAM CHOWDER

Clams are available fresh or canned. Chowders, fritters and the like work well with clams in any form. If using fresh clams, be sure they are alive when purchased. The shell will be tightly closed or will close when the shell is tapped. As is true with scallops, gentle cooking is the key to preventing the rubbery consistency often associated with clams.

Nova Scotians don't argue about "Manhattan" or "New England" clam chowder. We know we have the best. You can choose between a recipe for a traditional Maritime clam chowder and a surprising low-fat version that keeps all the flavor.

1 tbsp	butter	15 mL
1	medium onion, chopped	1
2 cups	diced potatoes	500 mL
2 cups	combined clam liquor and water	500 mL
2 cups	clams	500 mL
½ tsp	salt	2 mL
	Fresh ground pepper to taste	
2 cups	milk	500 mL
2 tsp	butter	10 mL
1 tbsp	chopped fresh parsley	15 mL
4	slices of bacon cooked crisp, chopped	4

In a saucepan over medium heat, melt the butter and sauté the onions until transparent. Add the potatoes, with the clam liquor and water combined to make 2 cups (500 mL). Cover and simmer for 10 to 15 minutes or until potatoes are tender. Add clams, salt, pepper, milk and butter. Simmer until mixture is hot, but do not allow to boil. Garnish with chopped parsley and crisp bacon.

Makes 4 to 6 servings.

LOW-FAT CLAM CHOWDER

2	medium potatoes	2
¼ cup	margarine	50 mL
½ cup	chopped onion	125 mL
½ cup	chopped green onion	125 mL
¼ cup	chopped green pepper	50 mL
¼ cup	all-purpose flour	50 mL
3½ cups	skim milk	875 mL
½ cup	clam juice	125 mL
2 cups	corn	500 mL
	Salt and freshly ground black pepper to taste	
¼ cup	fresh thyme or	50 mL
	1 tsp (5 mL) dried	
1 lb	clams, fresh or canned	500 g
2 tbsp	cooking sherry	25 mL

The word "chowder" orginated from the French "chaudière," a type of pot in which the dish was made.

Peel and dice potatoes and cook them over medium heat, in just enough water to cover. Drain potatoes. In a large stock pot, over medium heat, melt the margarine. Add the onions, green onion and green pepper and sauté for 5 to 6 minutes, stirring often. Add the flour and stir constantly for 1 minute. Slowly add the milk and clam juice and whisk until smooth. Add the corn, salt, pepper, thyme and clams and reduce the heat to low. Simmer until hot. Add the potatoes and sherry. Cook an additional 2 minutes and serve.

Makes 6 servings.

CHAPTER THREE

Salmon and Other Fin Fish

Lobster or salmon? Which is the king of seafood in Nova Scotia? If taste were the only measure, we think the result would be a tie. However, if beauty and an evocation of the romance of the sea were the criteria, salmon would win hands down. The Atlantic salmon, with its distinctive spotted tail and pink, succulent flesh, is prized by the sports fisherman and the connoisseur of fine dining alike. The real winner is the wild Atlantic salmon, which is born in fresh water, and then adapts to salt water, migrating to the open sea and returning to the rivers only to spawn. Very few of these fish, with their incredible deep flavor and beautiful, firm texture, are available in the market. However, this situation is changing year by year thanks to careful management of the stock, and someday the wild salmon may again be abundant. Happily, Nova Scotia and the other Maritime provinces are in the forefront of the aquaculture industry and are producing farm-raised salmon that have taste and texture similar to those of the wild variety. Atlantic salmon (unlike the Pacific salmon varieties) is a member of the same family as the species of trout that can also be found in the Nova Scotian fish markets. These include the freshwater brown, rainbow and cut throat, and the salt-water steelhead trout.

Salmon is so versatile that it can be poached, baked, broiled, grilled or steamed, with equally delicious results. The flesh is just fat enough to require little additional moisture, yet the flavor will also shine through the zestiest of sauces.

Salmon, of course, is not the only fresh fish available. We have also explored a variety of ways to cook the haddock, swordfish, shark and sole that are brought to market by the Nova Scotian fishing fleet. There are many ways to substitute one type of fish for another. Trout, salmon, Arctic char (also now being farm-raised) can often fill in for one another. Sole, ocean perch and flounder are similar enough to act as substitutes for one another, as are swordfish, blue shark and halibut. Of course, in dishes that feature a particular texture or color, the substitution will not work as well. But experimentation is fun and will expand your culinary repertoire. When preparing any fish, the general rule is to cook it for ten minutes for each inch (2.5 cm) of thickness to yield a moist result.

Freshness and careful handling are the key to preparing enjoyable seafood. Use a market that you trust, and look for firm flesh without a hint of off-odors. Fresh fish needs to be refrigerated as soon as possible after purchase. It should be kept in the coldest part of the refrigerator, well wrapped, and used within two days.

Each summer and fall, seafood festivals and suppers are hosted all over Nova Scotia. The North Shore Chowder challenge in River John is one such event. Here, every year, steaming cauldrons of chowder are presented for judging as the best on the North Shore. Each contestant uses sparklingly fresh fish, some vegetables, stock, milk or cream and secret herbs and spices. The judges never have an easy time choosing the best, but all enjoy the process. Not to be outdone, the summer residents of the South Shore village of Chester, built up in the early part of the century by summering Americans, have their own chowder festival. We are partial to the Chester event, since Heather has been asked to be a judge there. The Herring Chockers Picnic, held yearly on Tancook Island, honors the underused, beautifully striped, dark-fleshed fish that many assume is too "fishy" to enjoy. In fact, the mackerel is an ideal fish for the cook who is trying the piquant sauces so common in Mediterranean, Caribbean and South American cooking. Tomatoes, capers, olives, citrus fruits and hot peppers all are wonderful complements to the mackerel.

The culture of Nova Scotia is to a great extent defined by the fishing industry. The fishery fueled the economy during the decades of abundance, creating jobs for the fishermen themselves, the processors, the shipbuilders and more. The industry has struggled in recent years as the catch has dwindled, yet the fishing families have maintained their independence, toughness and a connection to the sea. They have opened markets for less commonly used species and have participated in conservation programs that are showing promising signs, restoring the hope that another generation of fishermen may yet be able to follow the tradition of their ancestors.

Grilled or broiled salmon lends itself to countless marinades and glazes. The following three recipes are some of our favorites.

GRILLED SALMON WITH DIJON MUSTARD AND HONEY MARINADE

The honey caramelizes when exposed to the heat of the grill or the broiler to produce a brown crust that keeps the fish moist. The addition of the slightly spicy, vinegary Dijon mustard cuts the sweetness of the honey.

4	filets of Atlantic salmon, 6 oz (180 g) each	4

Marinade

¼ cup	Dijon mustard	50 mL
¼ cup	fresh lemon juice	50 mL
¼ cup	liquid honey	50 mL

In a small bowl, whisk together Dijon mustard, lemon juice and honey until well blended.

Using two layers of foil, make four individual aluminum-foil trays with a rim. Pour 1 tbsp (15 mL) of marinade in each tray. Place a salmon fillet (skinned and deboned) in each tray and brush generously with marinade.

Grill 6 inches (15 cm) from coals on high heat or broil in oven for 6 to 8 minutes, watching carefully. Remove from heat if marinade starts to burn. Carefully remove fillets from trays and serve immediately with additional marinade to moisten.

Makes 4 servings.

SPICY MAPLE BROILED SALMON

The sauce makes a shiny sweet glaze that chars a little while cooking, which adds to the unusual maple flavor. Fresh ginger adds the spice. Fresh ginger root can be kept frozen and used without thawing first. In this recipe, it will give a superior result, compared with the powdered form.

⅓ cup	pure maple syrup	75 mL
½ cup	water	125 mL
4 tsp	peeled and minced ginger root	20 mL
2	cloves garlic, minced	2
¼ tsp	salt	1 mL
4	salmon fillets, 6 oz (180 g) each Salt and pepper	4

In a small saucepan over medium heat, combine maple syrup, water, ginger root, garlic and salt and heat until mixture reaches a gentle boil, stirring occasionally. Reduce heat to low and simmer until sauce is reduced to approximately ½ cup (125 mL). Cool.

Place salmon fillets on the broiler pan and season with salt and pepper. Broil in a preheated broiler about 4 inches (10 cm) from heat source, for 4 minutes. Remove from broiler, brush with sauce and broil again until the salmon flakes easily, about 6 more minutes.

Makes 4 servings.

The general rule of thumb for cooking fish is 10 minutes per inch (2.5 cm).

BROILED SALMON WITH TARRAGON BUTTER

Atlantic salmon weigh between 4 and 12 lbs (2 and 5 kg), although some grow to 40 lbs (18 kg). Salmon fillets and steaks and whole salmon lend themselves to being baked, broiled, poached, sautéed, grilled and microwaved.

Tarragon, with its mild anise-like taste, complements the richness of the salmon. Garnish with whole sprigs of fresh tarragon.

½ cup	butter	125 mL
1	small clove garlic, minced	1
1 tsp	lemon juice	5 mL
½ tsp	grated lemon rind	2 mL
1 tbsp	finely chopped fresh tarragon or 1 tsp (5 mL) dry tarragon soaked, 30 minutes in 2 tbsp (25 mL) of warm water, drain excess water	15 mL
4	6-oz (180-g) salmon fillets	4

In a saucepan over medium heat, melt the butter and stir in the garlic, lemon juice and lemon rind, mixing well. Brush salmon fillets with some of the lemon butter and grill or broil as in previous two recipes. Remove from grill, add tarragon to remaining butter and spoon over salmon.

Makes 4 servings.

OVEN-POACHED SALMON WITH YOGURT DILL SAUCE

Because many home cooks do not have a fish poacher, they have not been able to try this wonderful method of preparing whole fish. Our technique of pouring wine and lemon juice over a whole salmon and wrapping it in foil before baking produces a poached-style, moist fish. Dill is a traditional Northern European garnish for salmon.

¼ cup	olive oil	50 mL
4 to 5 lbs	whole salmon, scaled, head and tail removed	2 kg
6	green onions, chopped	6
¼ cup	fresh lemon juice	50 mL
½ cup	dry white wine	125 mL
12	whole black peppercorns	12
	Fresh dill and lemon curls	

Spread two large sheets of heavy-duty foil, shiny side up, on a baking sheet and coat with 1 tbsp (15 mL) of the olive oil. Place the fish on the foil. Sprinkle inside cavity of the fish with half of the green onions and half of the lemon juice. Sprinkle the remaining lemon juice, oil, wine, peppercorns and green onions around the fish. Fold the foil around the fish, closing tightly at the top, leaving a space between the foil and the salmon. Bake in a preheated 350°F (180°C) oven for 45 minutes.

Remove from the oven and open the foil. If serving warm, allow to cool enough to handle. Carefully remove the skin and open the two halves of the salmon so they lie flat. Reach for the center bone and pull from one end. The smaller side bones will lift away. If serving cold, reseal the foil after the fish has cooled and refrigerate for up to 1 day.

Refrigerate fresh seafood as soon as possible after purchase; place in the coldest part of the refrigerator and cook within two days of purchasing.

Dill Sauce

1½ cups	plain yogurt*	375 mL
4½ tsp	lemon juice	22 mL
2	finely chopped green onions	2
1 tsp	chopped fresh dill	5 mL
	Salt and pepper to taste	

In a small saucepan, combine the yogurt, lemon juice, green onions and fresh dill. Season with salt and pepper to taste. Over medium high heat, cook the sauce until hot but do not allow to boil. Remove from heat and serve immediately with hot salmon or cool and serve with the cold salmon.

Garnish with fresh dill sprigs and lemon curls.

*Sour cream may be substituted for the yogurt.

Makes 8 to 10 servings.

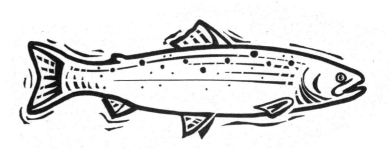

SALMON CAKES WITH CUCUMBER SAUCE

*Salmon cakes are a great way to use left-over salmon.
These cakes and the relish-like sauce make a tasty addition
to a festive outdoor event. Pernod or any other anise-
flavored liqueur is not essential but it does add zip.*

Salmon Cakes

1 lb	fresh cooked salmon	500 g
2	eggs	2
2 tbsp	lemon juice	25 mL
2	green onions, finely chopped	2
1 tbsp	minced parsley	15 mL
1½ cups	soft bread crumbs (3 slices)	375 mL
	Salt and pepper to taste	

In a food processor fitted with a metal blade, process the salmon,
eggs, lemon juice, green onions, parsley and bread crumbs until
well combined. Season with salt and pepper to taste. Using ¼ cup
(50 mL) as a measure, form into cakes. Sauté in hot oil until golden
brown on both sides and heated through. Divide evenly and place
on warmed plates. Serve with Cucumber Sauce.

Makes 4 servings.

Cucumber Sauce

2	eggs, hard-boiled	2
1	small cucumber, peeled, seeded and chopped	1
1	small onion, chopped	1
1 tbsp	chopped fresh dill	15 mL
1 tbsp	Pernod (optional)	15 mL
3 tbsp	vegetable oil	45 mL
¼ cup	red wine vinegar	50 mL

In a food processor fitted with a metal blade, process eggs, cucumber, onion and dill until finely chopped. Add the Pernod (optional), oil and vinegar and process until well combined. Chill.

Makes 2 cups (500 mL).

Seafood Substitutions:

In most recipes the following substitutions will work:
trout: Atlantic salmon, Arctic char, steelhead salmon
haddock: cod, cusk, ocean catfish, Boston bluefish, hake, turbot, monkfish
sole: ocean perch, grenadier, flounder
swordfish: blue shark, mako shark, halibut, tuna
lobster: crab, monkfish, pink shrimp, scallops
mussels: clams

SMOKED SALMON SALAD

*The traditional combination of smoked salmon, capers
and red onion is served here as the main ingredients for
an interesting salad instead of being paired with cream
cheese and a bagel.*

6 tbsp	extra-virgin olive oil	90 mL
3 tbsp	balsamic vinegar	45 mL
1 tsp	Dijon mustard	5 mL
	Salt and freshly ground pepper	
6 cups	mixed salad greens	1.5 L
8 oz	smoked salmon	250 g
4½ tsp	capers	22 mL
32	cherry tomatoes	32
1	small red onion, peeled and thinly sliced	1

Whisk the oil, vinegar and mustard in a bowl until the dressing is
emulsified. Season with salt and freshly ground pepper.

Wash the greens and spin or roll dry in a tea towel. Toss with
enough of the dressing to coat. Divide among 4 plates. Place equal
amounts of the salmon on each plate. Sprinkle more dressing and
the capers on top. Finally, garnish with cherry tomatoes and red
onion.

Makes 4 servings.

SMOKED SALMON WITH POTATO PANCAKES

Our last cookbook, The Taste of Nova Scotia Cookbook, *included a recipe for smoked salmon as an appetizer. Many readers have told us it's their favorite in the book. Here are two variations on the theme. The first is easy to make ahead. The potato pancakes are crunchy and should be served hot from the skillet. The sliced salmon is simple to use and makes a beautiful presentation. Garnish either dish with sprigs of fresh dill and lemon slices.*

1	small onion, quartered	1
3	baking potatoes, peeled (1¼ lb / 625 g)	3
2	eggs	2
3½ tsp	flour	17 mL
½ tsp	salt	2 mL
⅛ tsp	pepper	0.5 mL
	Vegetable oil (for cooking)	
8 oz	smoked salmon	250 g
½ cup	sour cream	125 mL
¼ cup	chopped fresh chives or dill	50 mL
	Lemon slices	

In a food processor fitted with the shredder blade, or with a hand grater, alternately shred the onion quarters and potatoes. Place in a colander, and with your hands, squeeze out as much moisture as possible. Discard the liquid. Transfer the onion and potato mixture to a large bowl and mix in the eggs, flour, salt and pepper. Let stand for 5 minutes and then pour off any liquid.

In a large frying pan over high heat, heat ¼ inch (6 mm) of oil until hot, not smoking. Measure ¼ cup (50 mL) of the potato/onion mixture per pancake into the hot oil, leaving about 1 inch (2.5 cm) between each cake. Flatten each slightly. Fry for 3 minutes, or until browned with crisp edges. With slotted spoon, turn and fry for 2 to 3 more minutes, until crisp and golden. Place pancakes on paper towels to drain. Repeat with remaining mixture, being careful to remove any cooked bits from the pan and adding more oil as needed.

Divide pancakes evenly onto each of 4 plates. For each serving, use ¼ of the smoked salmon. Place it on top of the pancakes, and top with the sour cream. Sprinkle with chopped chives or fresh dill and lemon slices.

Makes 4 servings.

Nova Scotia smoked salmon is either hot or cold smoked, with each producer having its own secret combination of the amount of salt, the woods used to impart the flavor and the smoking time. Unlike lox, a Scottish technique of heavily salting the salmon before smoking to preserve the fish prior to refrigeration, Nova Scotia smoked salmon uses salt for flavor only, not as a preservative, and is therefore more delicately flavored and needs to be kept frozen or refrigerated.

TWO-SALMON TARTAR

Salmon tartar is a silky spread that makes a very pretty appetizer. It uses both a mild-flavored fresh fillet and diced slices of wood-smoked salmon, which blend beautifully.

2 tbsp	regular or light mayonnaise	25 mL
1 tbsp	lemon juice	15 mL
½ tsp	capers, chopped	2 mL
¼ tsp	pepper	1 mL
	Dash of hot pepper sauce	
	Pinch of hot pepper flakes	
¼ lb	fresh salmon fillet	125 g
¼ lb	smoked salmon	125 g
	Fresh dill	

In a bowl, combine mayonnaise, lemon juice, capers, pepper, hot pepper sauce and hot pepper flakes. Finely chop the fresh and smoked salmon. Gently mix this into mayonnaise mixture. Serve on crackers or breads. Garnish with sprigs of fresh dill.

Makes about 1 cup (250 mL).

SMOKED MACKEREL PÂTÉ

Smoked mackerel is a favorite local seafood treat. This pâté, served on crisp crackers or lightly toasted slices of baguette, is a party dish that will disappear quickly.

1 lb	smoked mackerel (2 fillets)	500 g
4 oz	cream cheese, softened	125 g
1 tsp	Dijon mustard	5 mL
1 tbsp	mayonnaise	15 mL
2 tbsp	finely chopped celery or onion	25 mL
1 tbsp	finely chopped parsley	15 mL

Remove the skin and any bones from the smoked mackerel fillets. Cut into chunks and put in a food processor. Add cream cheese, mustard and mayonnaise, celery or onion and parsley and process until smooth.

Remove from the processor and refrigerate in a closed container for several hours or overnight until firm. Shape into a ball and garnish with fresh parsley. Serve with wafer crackers or toast points.

Makes 2 cups.

Mackerel is another of the underused and under-appreciated fish that many stay away from as too "fishy"— which is too bad since the somewhat stronger, but delicious, taste does very well with the punchy sauces of olives, capers, herbs and spices that the home cook is working with in today's kitchen.

PAN-FRIED HADDOCK WITH LEMON BUTTER

Pan frying can produce a non-greasy, crisp, light fish.
You may think that dredging the fish in flour and then
dipping it in the egg is backwards, but this reverse
process is what creates the crispy finish.

1½ tsp	butter	7 mL
1	clove garlic, minced	1
1 tsp	lemon juice	5 mL
¼ cup	butter	50 mL
½ tsp	lemon rind	2 mL
½ tsp	white pepper	2 mL
	Salt to taste	
1	egg, beaten	1
1 tbsp	water	15 mL
4	5-oz (150-g) haddock fillets	4
½ cup	seasoned flour*	125 mL

Lemon Butter: In a small saucepan over low heat, melt the 1½ tsp (7 mL) butter and sauté the garlic until soft, not browned, about 3 minutes. Add the lemon juice, and cook an additional 1 minute. Remove from heat and set aside. In a small bowl, cream the butter, lemon rind, pepper and salt. Add the garlic mixture, blending until smooth. Cover and refrigerate for at least 2 hours or overnight. After the butter has cooled for several hours, it may be shaped into a roll or pressed into a mold for serving. Chill until ready to serve.

In a shallow dish, blend the beaten egg and water. Put the seasoned flour in another shallow dish. Press the rinsed and patted-dry haddock fillets into the flour. Then dip them in the beaten egg mixture. Fry at high heat in good quality cooking oil until fish is flaky and has a golden brown crust. Serve immediately with lemon butter.

Season ½ cup (125 mL) all-purpose flour with ½ tsp (2 mL) salt and ¾ tsp (3 mL) freshly ground black pepper.

Makes 4 servings.

Suggested Cooking Methods for Seafood:

Selecting the proper cooking technique for the type of seafood chosen will provide the best results.

Poaching and Steaming: Arctic char, trout, halibut, mussels, scallops, salmon, steelhead, cusk, Boston bluefish, cod, haddock, sole, ocean perch, turbot, grenadier

Baking: Arctic char, trout, halibut, mussels, scallops, salmon, steelhead, cusk, Boston bluefish, cod, haddock, sole, ocean perch, turbot, grenadier, blue shark, mako shark, oysters, swordfish

Broiling and Barbecuing: Arctic char, trout, halibut, mussels, scallops, salmon, steelhead, cusk, Boston bluefish, cod, haddock, sole, ocean perch, turbot, grenadier, blue shark, mako shark, oysters, swordfish

Microwaving: Arctic char, trout, halibut, mussels, scallops, salmon, steelhead, cusk, Boston bluefish, cod, haddock, sole, ocean perch, turbot, grenadier

Stir-frying: Arctic char, trout, halibut, mussels, scallops, salmon, steelhead, cusk, blue shark, mako shark, oysters, swordfish

STEAMED HADDOCK WITH LOBSTER NEWBURG SAUCE

Enjoy elegant, rich Lobster Newburg over steamed haddock. This combination of shellfish and white fish complement each other wonderfully. Steaming retains moisture and keeps the fish light and flaky. The Newburg sauce is also excellent over cooked pasta such as linguine or fettucini.

3	egg yolks	3
1½ cups	light cream or milk	375 mL
1 tbsp	butter	15 mL
8 oz	lobster meat, chopped	250 g
1 tbsp	butter	15 mL
1 tbsp	all-purpose flour	15 mL
¼ cup	sherry	50 mL
1 tbsp	chopped fresh basil	15 mL
¾ tsp	freshly ground black pepper	3 mL
4	6-oz (180-g) boneless haddock fillets	4
4	sprigs of fresh dill	4
4	lemon or lime wedges	4

Newburg Sauce: In a bowl, whisk together the egg yolks and cream. You will require two skillets.

In one skillet, over medium heat, melt 1 tbsp (15 mL) of the butter and sauté the chopped lobster meat until hot. Remove from heat. Reduce heat, and in the second skillet, melt 1 tbsp (15 mL) butter, add 1 tbsp (15 mL) all-purpose flour, stirring constantly until the flour has browned, forming a roux. Remove from heat and add the egg and cream mixture to the roux, whisking until completely blended and smooth. Stir in the sherry, basil and pepper and add lobster meat. Stir over low heat until desired thickness is reached.

In a steamer, arrange haddock and sprinkle with fresh dill and the juice of the lemon or lime wedge. Cover and cook for 5 to 7 minutes or until the fish flakes easily when tested with a fork. Carefully transfer the haddock to plates and top with hot Newburg sauce.

Makes 4 servings.

SOLE AND SALMON ROULADES WITH DILL SAUCE

Roulade, the combination of a few ingredients rolled and sliced for a pretty presentation, is especially easy to make with fish since it is easy to roll. The pink salmon, white sole and green parsley and dill is lovely when cut and is presented in a spiral design. Drizzle the sauce over the plate before setting the fish roulade on it, so the colors of the roulade will show.

4	5-oz (150-g) sole fillets	4
2	6-oz (180-g) salmon fillets	2
2 tsp	chopped fresh dill	10 mL
4 tsp	chopped fresh parsley	20 mL
2 tsp	butter	10 mL

To make roulades, place the sole fillets on a flat surface. Carefully slice through the salmon fillets diagonally to form two thinner fillets. Place a salmon fillet on top of each sole fillet. Sprinkle each fillet with ½ tsp (2 mL) fresh chopped dill and 1 tsp (5 mL) fresh chopped parsley. Roll each fillet into a pinwheel. Cut each pinwheel into 3 or 4 equal sections. Place each pinwheel section (roulade) cut side down in a microwave-safe dish. Top each roulade with a dot of butter. Cover and microwave on high for 6 to 8 minutes or until fish is opaque in the center of each roulade. Remove roulade from dish and set aside on a warmed plate.

Dill Sauce

¼ cup	white wine	50 mL
1 tsp	chopped fresh dill	5 mL
½ cup	heavy cream (35%)	125 mL
2 tbsp	butter	25 mL

Strain remaining cooking liquid from roulade into a small saucepan
and place over medium heat. Add the white wine, fresh chopped dill
and heavy cream. Heat through—do not allow to boil—and add the
butter. Continue to cook, reducing until sauce has thickened.
Remove from heat and divide sauce evenly onto 4 serving plates.
Place 3 to 4 roulades on top of the sauce and garnish with fresh dill.
Serve with your favorite rice and green vegetable.

Makes 4 servings.

TOMATO-TOPPED SOLE

Halibut, sole and flounder are all flat fish, with eyes on one side of the head. They have mild-flavored white flesh. Flounder and sole are more delicate than halibut, and need a lighter, more subtle sauce. Halibut is firmer and can handle more piquant seasoning.

Most fish can be successfully cooked in the microwave. This one can go from the refrigerator to the table in 10 minutes, a real meal on the run.

2	5-oz (150-g) sole fillets	2
2	medium ripe tomatoes, sliced ½ inch (1 cm) thick	2
1 tsp	olive oil	5 mL
1 tsp	lemon juice	5 mL
1 tbsp	chopped fresh dill, basil or parsley (or ¼ tsp/1 mL dried) Freshly ground black pepper	15 mL

Microwave Method: Arrange tomato slices on a microwave-safe shallow dish or plate. Cover tomatoes with the fish and drizzle with oil and lemon juice. Sprinkle with the fresh or dried herb and season with black pepper. Cover with plastic wrap, venting one corner. Microwave on high power for 3 minutes or until fish is almost opaque and flakes easily when tested with a fork. Let rest for 1 minute before serving, draining any excess liquid.

Oven Method: In a shallow baking dish, arrange fish and cover with the sliced tomatoes. Drizzle with oil and lemon juice. Sprinkle with fresh dill and pepper to taste. Bake in a preheated 400°F (200°C) oven for 12 minutes or until fish is opaque and flakes easily when tested with a fork.

Makes 2 servings.

TROUT ON STIR-FRIED VEGETABLES

Use freshwater or rainbow trout. The diced vegetables called for here are the traditional "aromatics" used as the base for many dishes, including soups and stews.

4	trout, heads removed	4
	Salt and freshly ground pepper	
¼ cup	butter	50 mL
½ cup	diced carrots	125 mL
½ cup	diced celery	125 mL
½ cup	chopped onion	125 mL
½ cup	diced leek	125 mL
1 cup	snow peas	250 mL
2 cups	bean sprouts	500 mL
	Salt and freshly ground black pepper	
¼ cup	white wine	50 mL
4 tsp	lemon juice	20 mL

Wash trout. Pat it dry and season with salt and pepper. In a large Dutch oven, melt butter and sauté the carrots, celery, onions and leeks for 5 to 7 minutes. Add the snow peas, and cover and simmer for 1 or 2 minutes. Stir in the bean sprouts. Season with salt and pepper to taste. Arrange trout on top of partially cooked vegetables. In a small bowl, blend the wine and lemon juice and pour over the trout and vegetables. Cover tightly, and bake in a preheated 400°F (200°C) oven for 10 to 12 minutes or until the fish flakes easily when tested with a fork. To serve, remove top skin and brush with melted butter. Garnish with lemon slices and fresh chives.

Makes 4 servings.

Trout is another popular sport fish, like its relative the salmon. Most trout are freshwater, but some are found in the salty ocean. Some species are called "salmon-trout," or steelhead salmon, adding to an identity crisis. The larger fish can be filleted and cooked like salmon. The smaller brook or speckled trout are best cooked whole.

GRILLED SWORDFISH STEAKS

Shark as a seafood has grown in popularity in recent years. Blue and mako are the two varieties of shark found in the waters of the north Atlantic. They are commonly harvested from July to October, when the warmer water temperatures move their food supply north to our waters.

Swordfish is another local favorite in Nova Scotia. The steak needs to be ¾ to 1 inch (2 to 2.5 cm) in thickness for the best results on the grill. The citrusy marinade gives a piquant bite that can be enhanced even further by adding a few red pepper flakes or finely chopped hot green pepper such as jalapeño.

2 lbs	swordfish steaks, ¾ to 1 inch thick (2 to 2.5 cm) thick	1 kg

Marinade

¼ cup	soy sauce	50 mL
¼ cup	orange juice	50 mL
2 tbsp	tomato sauce or ketchup	25 mL
1 tbsp	lemon juice	15 mL
1	clove garlic, chopped	1
2 tbsp	chopped fresh parsley	25 mL
½ tsp	dried oregano	2 mL
½ tsp	ground black pepper	2 mL

Wash steaks under running water and pat dry. Place in a large Ziplock storage bag.

Marinade: In a small bowl, whisk together the soy sauce, orange juice, tomato sauce, lemon juice, garlic, parsley, oregano and pepper until well blended. Pour over swordfish steaks and refrigerate for 2 hours, turning the bag over once while marinating.

Place the steaks on a greased broiler or barbecue rack, 4 to 5 inches (10 to 12 cm) from the heat source. Baste and cook for 8 minutes. Turn, baste and cook an additional 5 minutes or until the fish flakes easily with a fork. Remove from grill and serve immediately.

Makes 6 servings.

SHARK KEBOBS

Shark is a great fish for the barbecue, as it retains its moisture over the high heat and its firm flesh stays whole even when cut into small cubes and threaded on skewers. Not as well known for grilling as swordfish or tuna, it is an excellent choice and deserves to be used more widely.

1 lb	shark fillets or steaks	500 g
½ cup	lemon juice	125 mL
½ cup	olive oil	125 mL
2 tbsp	chopped fresh parsley	25 mL
1 tsp	dry mustard	5 mL
1	clove garlic, minced	1
¼ tsp	freshly ground pepper	1 mL
	Salt to taste	
	Mushrooms	
	Cherry tomatoes	

Cut shark into 1-inch (2.5-cm) cubes. Place them in a Ziplock storage bag. In a small bowl, whisk together the lemon juice, oil, parsley, dry mustard, garlic, salt and pepper. Pour the marinade over the shark in the bag, stirring to coat, and refrigerate for 45 minutes.

To assemble kebob, thread shark alternately with mushrooms and cherry tomatoes (or other vegetables) on a metal skewer or wooden one soaked in water for at least 1 hour. Reserve remaining marinade for basting the shark as it cooks. Grill 4 inches (10 cm) from heat source for about 10 minutes, turning to brown all sides.

Makes 4 servings.

SHARK WITH TOMATO AND GARLIC SAUCE

The firm-fleshed shark stands up to this full-flavored, Greek-influenced marinade and piquant tomato sauce flavored with fruity olive oil. Quick cooking keeps the fish moist. Fresh herbs are important since the sauce doesn't cook for very long and dried herbs won't have time to release their flavors.

4	5-oz (150-g) servings of shark, monktail or halibut	4

Marinade

¼ cup	extra-virgin olive oil	50 mL
	Zest from 1 lemon	
	Juice from 1 lemon	
1 tbsp	finely chopped Italian parsley	25 mL
1 tbsp	finely chopped fresh basil	25 mL
½ tsp	freshly ground black pepper	2 mL

In a mixing bowl, whisk together all the marinade ingredients. Place fish in a large Ziplock storage bag and pour in marinade. Seal and turn to ensure the fish is well coated. Refrigerate for 1 to 2 hours before cooking.

Tomato and Garlic Sauce

2 tbsp	extra-virgin olive oil	25 mL
4	garlic cloves, finely chopped	4
2	shallots, finely diced	2
4	anchovy fillets, finely chopped	4
¼ cup	dry white wine	50 mL
4 cups	chopped fresh tomatoes, peeled and seeded	1 L
1 tsp	chopped fresh oregano	5 mL
	Salt and pepper to taste	
2 tbsp	extra-virgin olive oil	25 mL
2 tbsp	dry white wine	25 mL

In a large skillet or frying pan, heat the olive oil, and add the garlic, shallots and anchovies. Sauté until shallot is translucent. Deglaze the pan with the white wine and add the tomatoes, oregano, salt and pepper. Simmer for about 5 minutes to cook the tomatoes. Remove from heat, transfer to a food processor and purée until smooth. Reserve.

Remove the fish from the marinade and pat dry. In a large frying pan, heat the olive oil over high heat, and put the fish into the hot pan. Cook on each side for 2 minutes. Remove from pan and put in a baking pan. Bake in a preheated 350°F (180°C) oven until the fish flakes easily when tested with a fork, about 6 to 8 minutes. Take care not to overcook. Deglaze the same frying pan by adding the white wine and 2 tbsp (25 mL) of the marinade. Add the reserved tomato sauce and reheat. Pour the sauce over the cooked fish and serve.

Makes 4 servings.

SOLOMON GUNDY

Nova Scotians usually serve squares of herring with slices of raw onion, placed on a cracker or piece of toast and garnished with a tiny pickled red pepper. Other serving suggestions for Solomon Gundy include putting it in a tossed salad or on a bed of lettuce with orange pieces and other fruit.

From the Lunenburg County area of Nova Scotia's South Shore comes an appetizer of marinated herring commonly called Solomon Gundy. Salt herring is poached in a mixture of onions, vinegar, pickling spice and sugar. You can purchase it already prepared or have the satisfaction of making your own.

3	whole salt herring	3
1 tbsp	mixed pickling spice	15 mL
1½ cups	white vinegar	375 mL
½ cup	granulated sugar	125 mL
4	medium onions, sliced	4

Remove heads and tails from herring. Soak herring in cold water for 12 hours or overnight, changing water once or twice. Thoroughly clean and skin the herring, taking care to remove all bones. Cut into 1-inch (2.5-cm) squares. Tie the pickling spice in a cheesecloth bag. In a large saucepan, combine the vinegar and sugar. Add the spice bag and boil for 5 minutes. Cool. In a large glass container, alternately layer the herring and onion slices. Pour the cooled marinade over the herring. If you want a spicier taste, add the spice bag to the mixture. Keep refrigerated.

CHAPTER FOUR

MEATS AND POULTRY

Despite showing its face to the sea, Nova Scotia is home to many small family farms that have provided produce, dairy products and meat to the region since the days of the first settlers in the 1600s. The Acadians brought expert techniques of dairy farming and poultry raising, and the Scots carried the art of raising sheep across to the western side of the Atlantic. The Native Mi'kmaqs were expert hunters who used the venison, rabbits, pheasant, turkeys and ducks that teemed in abundance in the forests and near the shore. These days the farmers are also experimenting by raising the newer, more exotic animals such as emu, partridge, grouse and quail. Many of these products are now available in Nova Scotia's ever-growing number of fine restaurants, farmers' markets and higher-end groceries.

The meat and poultry sold locally by farmers are produced on farms that have changed with the times and use the technological advances of the farming industry. The result is a top-quality product that is very much a combination of time-tested tradition and new-age techniques.

The village of Kingston, in the Annapolis Valley of western Nova Scotia, is right in the middle of the most active dairy- and fruit-farming area of the province. The second Saturday of July is Kingston's biggest day of the year, when the Kingston Steer Barbecue takes over the town and brings residents and visitors together for an active day of parades, milking contests, food and plant sales, and a big town dance. One of the most exciting competitions on Steer Barbecue day is a heavy-horse pull, where teams of huge draft horses compete to see which can pull the most weight in the fastest time. In some years the winning teams have pulled more than 9,000 pounds (4000 kg). Of course, the day is defined by the smell of barbecued beef that cooks for hours on a spit in the middle of things. Well over 1,500 will eat the succulent beef, along with the dozens of loaves of bread baked by the expert bakers of the community, and a half-ton (450 kg) of cole slaw, potatoes and vegetables fresh from the farm.

NOVA SCOTIA CHICKEN STIR-FRY

Great care must be taken in handling raw chicken. Any utensils, cutting boards and knives used to work with raw poultry need to be well washed with hot soapy water before being used again.

A change of pace from many chicken dishes, this stir-fry uses a variety of vegetables that are quickly cooked to retain their color and texture. Use good-quality soy sauce that has not been sweetened. You can be creative with the vegetables—use broccoli, green beans or any others that strike your fancy.

1½ tsp	dry sherry	7 mL
1 tsp	vegetable oil	5 mL
¼ tsp	salt	1 mL
	Ground black pepper to taste	
1 tbsp	soy sauce	15 mL
½ tsp	granulated sugar	2 mL
1 tbsp	vegetable oil	15 mL
6 oz	fresh chicken breast, sliced	180 g
2 to 3	slices of fresh ginger root	2 to 3
1	small zucchini, sliced	1
2	small carrots, peeled and sliced	2
1 cup	sliced mushrooms	250 mL
1	small red onion, sliced	1
1 cup	snow peas, ends trimmed	250 mL
1	clove garlic, chopped	1
¾ tsp	cornstarch	3 mL
4 tsp	chicken stock	20 mL

In a small bowl, mix together sherry, oil, salt, pepper, soy sauce and sugar. Set aside. Heat a wok or large fry pan and add 1 tbsp (15 mL) oil. Add the chicken slices and ginger and sauté for 1 minute. Add vegetables and garlic and sauté for 1 minute. Add sherry mixture and bring to a boil. Blend the cornstarch into the chicken stock until smooth. Add to stir-fry mixture and stir for 30 seconds.

Serve immediately over rice or noodles.

Makes 2 servings.

GRILLED CHICKEN AND SPINACH SALAD WITH BALSAMIC VINAIGRETTE

*Grilled chicken breasts on a Caesar salad appear on
many menus these days—it's a salad that can serve as a
filling meal. Our combination of grilled chicken breast
and wonderful crunchy spinach in a slightly sweet
vinaigrette is a unique variation on the chicken Caesar.*

Dressing

½ cup	liquid honey	125 mL
½ cup	olive oil	125 mL
⅓ cup	balsamic vinegar	75 mL
1 tbsp	Dijon mustard	15 mL
2 tsp	chopped fresh parsley	10 mL
2 tsp	chopped red onion	10 mL
2 tsp	chopped fresh chives	10 mL
2 tsp	chopped red pepper	10 mL

Salad

4	6-oz (180-g) boneless chicken breasts	4
8 oz	fresh spinach	250 g
2	fresh oranges, peeled and sectioned into pieces	2
1	small red onion, sliced	1
4	fresh mushrooms, sliced	4
1	red pepper, diced	1

Dressing: In a bowl, whisk the honey, oil, vinegar and mustard until well blended and smooth. Add remaining ingredients. Whisk until blended. Chill until serving.

Salad: Grill chicken breasts and chill. Cut them into slices prior to serving.

Wash spinach and trim ends. In a medium-sized bowl, combine spinach, sectioned oranges, red onion, mushrooms and red pepper. Add vinaigrette and toss. Divide salad on individual plates and arrange chilled sliced chicken on top.

Makes 4 servings.

TURKEY POT PIE

A winner in the comfort-food department. There is something special about any dish that uses freshly made dumplings or biscuits—and these are easy to make. Save some time by using a food processor to make the dough. Just be sure to combine the butter with the rest of the dry ingredients by pulsing, not mixing, so the mixture stays coarse and the dumplings remain tender.

⅓ cup	butter	75 mL
2 cups	quartered mushrooms	500 mL
¼ cup	all-purpose flour	50 mL
1 cup	chicken stock	250 mL
2 cups	milk	500 mL
½ tsp	dried thyme	2 mL
¼ tsp	Tabasco sauce	1 mL
	Salt and pepper to taste	
4 cups	cooked, diced turkey or chicken	1 L
1½ cups	diced, cooked carrots	375 mL
1 cup	cooked peas	250 mL

Northern woodlands once teemed with wild turkeys that are making a comeback in the less-populated parts of Canada and the United States. The domestic turkey made a very long journey from Mexico, where the Aztecs raised them, to Europe, and back to North America to breed with the wild turkeys in the late 1600s. The breeders today are producing smaller (10–12 lbs/ 4.5–5 kg) birds that can be used by a family without the need to invite a dozen friends and relations.

In a large saucepan, melt the butter. Add the mushrooms and sauté for 2 to 3 minutes. Sprinkle the mushrooms with flour and continue to sauté for 5 minutes. Stir frequently, and do not brown. Add chicken stock and milk. Stir to combine and bring to a boil. Reduce heat. Add the thyme, Tabasco sauce, salt and pepper. Simmer for 10 minutes, stirring occasionally. Add diced turkey and vegetables to the sauce, stirring to combine. Spoon the turkey mixture in a greased 12-cup (3-L) casserole dish.

Dumpling Crust

1 cup	all-purpose flour	250 mL
2 tsp	baking powder	10 mL
¼ tsp	salt	1 mL
1 tbsp	chopped fresh parsley, or ½ tsp (2 mL) dried	15 mL

1 tbsp	chopped fresh dill or	15 mL
	½ tsp (2 mL) dried	
⅓ cup	cold butter	75 mL
½ cup	milk	125 mL

In a mixing bowl, blend the flour, baking powder, salt, parsley and dill. Cut in the butter with a pastry blender or fork to form a coarse crumb. Add the milk, stirring just enough to combine. Turn dough out onto a floured surface and roll out to fit the top of the casserole dish. Place the dough directly on top of the turkey mixture and cut steam vents.

Bake in a preheated 400°F (200°C) oven for 30 to 35 minutes.

Makes 6 servings.

TURKEY PASTA SALAD

How to use leftover turkey is a challenge we all face. Does anyone ever buy a turkey that just makes one meal? Pasta salad loaded with vegetables and tossed with cold turkey is a delicious, healthy solution.

Dressing

¼ cup	vegetable oil	50 mL
½ cup	red wine vinegar	125 mL
1 tbsp	granulated sugar	15 mL
1 tbsp	grated Parmesan cheese	15 mL
1 tsp	dried basil	5 mL
1	clove garlic, minced	1
½ tsp	salt	2 mL

In a mixing bowl, combine all dressing ingredients. Whisk until well blended and smooth.

Salad

4 cups	cooked fusilli pasta (approximately 6 oz/180 g uncooked pasta)	1 L
3 cups	diced cooked turkey or chicken	750 mL
2 cups	chopped broccoli	500 mL
3	green onion stalks, diced	3
1	large carrot, diced	1
¼ cup	chopped fresh parsley	50 mL
1	large, firm tomato, chopped	1

In a large mixing bowl, combine the pasta, turkey, broccoli, green onions, carrot and parsley. Pour over the dressing and toss. Cover and refrigerate for 1 to 2 hours to blend the flavors. Mix in the chopped tomatoes just prior to serving.

Makes 6 to 8 servings.

APPLE CHICKEN SALAD

Cortland apples are excellent for salads and raw garnishes because they stay white when cut. Other varieties should be dipped in lemon juice to prevent browning.

This salad is notable for its variety of crunchy ingredients—apples, nuts and celery. It needs to be chilled after combining to blend the flavors. There is no reason to peel the apples and lose the bright red color. For a more substantial meal, this salad could be tossed with cooked macaroni or other small pasta.

3 cups	diced cooked chicken or turkey	750 mL
1 cup	diced celery	250 mL
2 cups	chopped, unpeeled red apples	500 mL
¼ cup	slivered almonds (optional)	50 mL
¼ tsp	salt	1 mL
⅛ tsp	freshly ground black pepper	0.5 mL
⅛ tsp	ground cinnamon	0.5 mL
2 tbsp	finely chopped green onion	25 mL
¼ cup	shredded carrots	50 mL
½ cup	mayonnaise*	125 mL

In a large mixing bowl, combine the chicken, celery, apple, almonds, salt, pepper, cinnamon, green onion and carrots. Add the mayonnaise and toss gently to coat the ingredients. Cover and chill for several hours before serving. Serve on a bed of lettuce leaves, garnished with thin strips of red pepper.

You can replace the mayonnaise with ¼ cup (50 mL) each of plain yogurt and light mayonnaise.

Makes 6 servings.

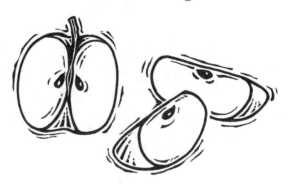

CHICKEN SOUP

No culinary culture in the world fails to have a regional version of the basic chicken soup. It has the remarkable ability to almost disappear in dishes calling for chicken stock as a base and to proclaim itself loud and clear when combined with a few vegetables and noodles.

To make this soup heartier, add more vegetables such as diced potatoes, parsnips and turnips.

4 quarts	water	4 L
2 lbs	chicken (wings, cut-up stewing hen or pieces)	1 kg
2	medium onions, diced	2
2	celery stalks, diced	2
4	carrots, sliced	4
½ cup	tomato paste	125 mL
1 tsp	salt	5 mL
2	whole bay leaves	2
12	black peppercorns	12
1 tsp	curry	5 mL
2	red apples, cored and diced	2

Put the water and chicken in a large stock pot or saucepan and bring to a boil over medium high heat. Reduce heat and simmer for 1 to 1½ hours until the meat starts to come away from the bones. Remove from heat and pour the stock through a colander. Put chicken stock in a glass bowl and refrigerate to cool. Remove the meat from the bones, discarding the skin. Cut the chicken into bite-sized pieces, and refrigerate. When the chicken broth has cooled, skim off the fat that has formed on the top. Put stock and chicken back into the cleaned stock pot and add the onion, celery, carrots, tomato paste, salt, bay leaves, peppercorns and curry. Cook over medium low heat until the vegetables are tender crisp. Add the diced apple and continue to cook for 10 minutes. Serve hot with fresh biscuits.

Makes 8 to 10 servings.

CHICKEN FRICOT

Fricot *is a French traditional hearty soup that combines meat and potatoes in a flavorful broth.*

The Acadian settlers brought this dish to our shores in the 1600s. Good fricot is appearing in restaurants where chefs are looking to old recipes for inspiration in developing new ones.

¼ cup	butter	50 mL
4 to 5 lbs	chicken legs or stewing hen, cut into pieces	2 kg
1 tsp	salt	5 mL
¼ tsp	black pepper	1 mL
1	large onion, coarsely diced	1
6 cups	boiling water	1.5 L
1 tbsp	dried savory	15 mL
3 cups	diced carrots	750 mL
3 cups	diced potatoes	750 mL

In a large heavy-bottomed saucepan or Dutch oven, melt the butter and cook the chicken pieces over medium heat for 30 minutes. Add the salt, pepper and onion and cook for 10 minutes, until the onion is soft. Add the boiling water and savory. Reduce heat and simmer for 20 minutes or until the chicken is tender and the meat begins to come away from the bones. There are two ways to proceed from this point.

The traditional way is to leave the meat on the bone and serve the soup bone-in. Add the carrots and potatoes. Increase the heat to medium and cook for 20 minutes. Reduce the heat to low and simmer for an additional 20 minutes. Serve hot.

A second way is to remove the chicken pieces from the pot and allow them to cool. Add the carrots and potatoes to the hot stock and simmer for 20 minutes. Meanwhile, remove the meat from the bones. Add the meat back to stock mixture and simmer an additional 20 minutes. Serve hot.

Makes 8 to 10 servings.

ROASTED CHICKEN WITH BLUEBERRY PEPPERCORN SAUCE

In Central and Eastern Europe, as in Nova Scotia, a wonderful, crisp roast chicken is the centerpiece of the family's Sunday dinner. This spicy-sweet blueberry sauce turns a simple roasted chicken into an elegant dish. Fluffy steamed rice is an excellent accompaniment.

1	roasted chicken	1
4 tsp	granulated sugar	20 mL
½ cup	white wine	125 mL
½ cup	chicken stock	125 mL
2 tsp	balsamic vinegar	10 mL
¾ tsp	whole pink peppercorns	3 mL
¼ cup	wild blueberries, fresh or frozen	50 mL
4 tsp	butter	20 mL
	Salt to taste	

Cut roasted chicken into quarters. In a warmed saucepan, add the sugar and stir until it melts. Add the wine, chicken stock, vinegar, peppercorns and blueberries. Increase the heat to medium high and reduce sauce by half. Whisk in the butter to thicken the sauce, taking care not to let it come to the boil. Season with salt to taste. Arrange quartered chicken on serving plates and top with sauce.

Makes 4 servings.

The smaller broiler fryers and roasters (under 3 lbs/1.4 kg) are the more tender chickens. The heavier roaster of 3 to 6 lbs (1.4 to 2.7 kg) has more fat and roasts very well. The older birds, labeled stewing chickens (or, sometimes, boiling fowl), have great flavor but tougher meat. They are good if cooked with a liquid in a stewed dish. There is a significant difference in taste in a free-range chicken, and the extra cost is worth incurring—at least at those times when roast chicken will be the centerpiece of the meal.

Marinated Beef Kebobs

Beef, especially the less tender cuts, benefits from marinating in the same way as fish or poultry. The marinade infuses the meat with flavors and additional moisture that keeps the beef cubes plump while grilling.

½ cup	vegetable oil	125 mL
2 tbsp	cider vinegar	25 mL
1 tsp	celery seed	5 mL
1 tbsp	finely chopped onion	15 mL
1	clove garlic, minced	1
¾ tsp	dried oregano	3 mL
¼ tsp	salt	1 mL
¼ tsp	freshly ground black pepper	1 mL
2 lbs	boneless beef	1 kg
	Mushroom caps	
	Zucchini slices	
	Red pepper cubes	

In a small mixing bowl, whisk together the oil, vinegar, celery seed, onion, garlic, oregano, salt and pepper. Cut the beef into 1½-inch (3-cm) cubes. Place beef cubes in a plastic Ziplock bag and pour in the marinade. Seal bag and refrigerate for 4 to 6 hours, turning the bag occasionally. Thread the marinated beef on either metal or soaked wooden skewers, alternating with the vegetables. Place on an oiled rack and grill over hot coals, or place under a preheated broiler for 10 to 15 minutes, turning and basting frequently.

Makes 6 servings.

ROAST BEEF

The traditional Sunday dinner roast. The roast can be rubbed before going in the oven with a variety of seasonings that will infuse the juices (and any gravy you make with them) with the herb and seasoning flavors.

3 lbs	roast of beef	1.5 kg
	(sirloin, rib, rump, round, sirloin tip)	

Herb Seasoning

1 tbsp	dried thyme	15 mL
1 tsp	dried rosemary	5 mL
1 tsp	dried sage	5 mL
1 tsp	salt	5 mL
1 tsp	black pepper	5 mL

Combine ingredients and rub on the meat before roasting.

Pepper Seasoning

2 tbsp	Dijon mustard	25 mL
1 tbsp	lemon juice	15 mL
1 tbsp	crushed black peppercorns	15 mL
½ tsp	dried oregano	2 mL

Combine ingredients and spread on the meat before roasting.

Dijon Seasoning

1 tbsp	Dijon mustard	15 mL
¼ cup	red wine	50 mL

Checking the internal temperature of a roast of beef with a meat thermometer is the most accurate measure of the degree of doneness. Insert the thermometer into the center of the roast, making sure it does not touch fat or bone. The internal temperature should be 140°F (60°C) for rare, 160°F (70°C) for medium and 170°F (75° C) for well done.

Spread the mustard on the roast, add the red wine and baste with the wine while roasting.

Place roast, fat side up, in a roasting pan. Season as desired. For a sirloin or rib roast, cook uncovered, in a preheated 325°F (160°C) oven. For rare, cook for 20 min/lb (45 min/kg); for medium, cook the roast 25 min/lb (55 min/kg); and for well done, roast for 30 to 35 min/lb (65 min/kg). For rump, round or sirloin tip roasts, reduce the oven temperature to 275°F (140°C) and cook only to the rare or medium doneness for best results at 40 min/lb (90 min/kg).

Makes 6 to 8 servings.

BEEF GOULASH

Goulash arrived with Central European settlers. Be sure that the beef simmers and doesn't boil. Slow cooking will tenderize the meat.

For a heartier meal, serve the goulash over buttered egg noodles.

2 tsp	vegetable oil	10 mL
1	medium onion, chopped	1
1 lb	stewing beef, cut into 1-inch (2.5-cm) cubes	500 g
¼ cup	all-purpose flour	50 mL
1	bottle amber or dark beer	1
¾ cup	water	175 mL
¼ cup	tomato paste	50 mL
1	medium green pepper, chopped	1
1 tsp	paprika	5 mL
¼ tsp	salt	1 mL
¼ tsp	freshly ground black pepper	1 mL
¼ tsp	dried marjoram	1 mL
¼ tsp	caraway seeds (optional)	1 mL
3	potatoes, peeled and cut into 1-inch (2.5-cm) cubes	3
½ cup	sour cream	125 mL
2 tbsp	chopped fresh parsley	25 mL

In a heavy-bottomed pot or Dutch oven, heat the oil over medium heat. Add the onion and sauté for 5 minutes. Add the stewing beef. Sprinkle on the flour, and stir until the meat is browned on all sides. Add the beer, water, tomato paste, green pepper, paprika, salt, pepper, marjoram and caraway seeds. Cover and simmer for 1½ hours or until the meat is tender. Do not cook too fast. Add the potatoes and cook for an additional 20 minutes. Remove 1 cup (250 mL) of the sauce from the pot, and allow it to cool slightly. Blend it with the sour cream. Return the sour cream mixture to the pot and stir well. Spoon goulash into heated bowls and garnish with chopped parsley.

Makes 4 servings.

TANGY MEAT LOAF

It is hard to imagine any home cook who does not have a favorite meat loaf recipe in his or her collection. This combination of ground beef, milk and rolled oats keeps the loaf moist. When working with any ground meat, whether patties or loaves, the key to tenderness is not to over-mix.

1 lb	lean ground beef	500 g
1	small onion, chopped	1
⅔ cup	rolled oats	150 mL
	Salt and pepper to taste	
2 tsp	dried summer savory	10 mL
1	egg	1
½ cup	milk	125 mL
¼ cup	tomato sauce or ketchup	50 mL

Topping

½ cup	brown sugar	125 mL
¼ cup	white vinegar	50 mL
½ tsp	dry mustard	2 mL
	Dash of Worcester sauce	

In a mixing bowl, blend the ground beef, onion, rolled oats, salt, pepper and summer savory. In a small bowl, lightly beat the egg and stir in the milk and tomato sauce. Stir into the meat mixture until well blended. Put in an 8-inch (20-cm) square baking pan.

Topping: In a small bowl, stir together the brown sugar, vinegar, mustard and Worcester sauce until smooth. Spoon it over the meat mixture and cook in a preheated 350°F (180°C) oven for 40 to 45 minutes or until there is no pinkness in the meat.

Makes 6 servings.

BEEF AND CHEDDAR PIE

The Belgians use beer and beef in their famous Carbonnade. The full-bodied Canadian beer, especially the locally produced amber or dark varieties, gives a rich, mahogany gravy.

1 lb	stewing beef, cut into ½-inch (1-cm) cubes	500 g
1 tbsp	all-purpose flour	15 mL
1 tbsp	vegetable oil	15 mL
1 tbsp	soy sauce	15 mL
1	clove garlic, minced	1
1½ tsp	mild chili powder	7 mL
½ tsp	salt	2 mL
½ cup	beer	125 mL
½ cup	diced green peppers	125 mL
1 lb	sharp or aged cheddar cheese, grated	500 g
	Single-crust pie pastry	
1	egg, beaten	1
1 tbsp	milk	15 mL

In a mixing bowl, toss the cubed beef and flour to coat evenly. In a saucepan, heat the vegetable oil. Add the beef and cook until browned on all sides. Add the soy sauce, garlic, chili powder and salt. Stir to combine and cook 5 minutes. Stir in the beer. Cover and simmer for 1 hour until the sauce has thickened. Add the green peppers. Pour meat mixture into a 6-cup (1.5-mL) casserole dish. Evenly spread the grated cheese over the beef mixture. Top with a pie crust rolled out to fit plate. Seal the edges, and cut several heat vents. In a small bowl, whisk together the egg and milk to form an egg wash. Brush the crust with the egg wash. Bake in a preheated 400°F (200°C) oven for 30 minutes or until crust is golden brown. Serve with a green side salad.

Makes 6 servings.

BEEF STEW WITH CARROT DUMPLINGS

Slow cooking with quite a bit of liquid tenderizes the stew beef and provides a rich gravy. We offer two different and unusual dumpling recipes to try. One is flecked green with parsley and the other has the surprising color and crunch of carrot.

2½ lbs	stewing beef	1 kg
⅓ cup	vegetable oil	75 mL
1	medium onion, chopped	1
1	clove garlic, minced	1
⅓ cup	seasoned all-purpose flour*	75 mL
2 tbsp	chopped fresh parsley	25 mL
½ tsp	dried savory	2 mL
½ tsp	dried thyme	2 mL
½ tsp	salt	2 mL
½ tsp	ground black pepper	2 mL
3¼ cups	water	800 mL
2	medium carrots, sliced	2
6	small onions, sliced	6
1	small rutabaga, diced	1

To make the seasoned flour, combine ⅓ cup (75 mL) all-purpose flour with ½ tsp (2 mL) salt and ¼ tsp (1 mL) ground black pepper.

In a Dutch oven or other large, heavy pot, heat the oil until very hot, but not smoking, over high heat. Add the beef and brown on all sides. Remove the meat and set aside. Reduce the heat to medium. Add the onions and garlic and sauté until the onions are transparent. Return the meat to the pot. Sprinkle with the seasoned flour and continue to cook, stirring occasionally, until the flour has browned. Add the water, parsley, savory, thyme, salt and pepper and bring to a boil. Reduce the heat to low and simmer, covered, for 45 minutes. Add the carrots, onions and rutabaga and cook an additional 20 minutes. Then add your choice of dumpling.

Carrot Dumplings

1½ cups	all-purpose flour	375 mL
1 tbsp	baking powder	15 mL
¼ tsp	salt	1 mL
3 tbsp	butter, melted	45 mL
2 tbsp	finely shredded carrot	25 mL
½ cup	milk	125 mL
1	egg, slightly beaten	1

In a mixing bowl, blend the flour, baking powder and salt. Stir in the melted butter and grated carrot. In a small mixing bowl, blend the milk and egg and add to the flour mixture, stirring to combine. This will make a fairly stiff dough that can be dropped by generous tablespoons on top of the hot stew. Cover and cook for 20 minutes. Do not peek, so the dumplings can steam.

Parsley Dumplings

1½ cups	all-purpose flour	375 mL
1 tbsp	baking powder	15 mL
¼ tsp	salt	1 mL
¼ cup	shortening	50 mL
3 tbsp	chopped fresh parsley	45 mL
¾ cup	milk	175 mL

In a mixing bowl, blend the flour, baking powder and salt. Cut in the shortening until the mixture resembles a coarse crumb. Add the chopped parsley. Add the milk to the dough and stir to form a soft dough, adding more milk if required. Drop a tablespoon at a time on top of the hot stew. Cook as above.

Makes 6 servings.

PORK CACCIATORE

*Cacciatore refers to a richly flavored dish cooked
with tomatoes, mushrooms and herbs.*

1 lb	boneless pork, leg or butt	500 g
	cut into 1-inch (2.5-cm) cubes	
	Salt and pepper to taste	
2 tbsp	olive oil	25 mL
⅔ cup	coarsely chopped onion	150 mL
2	cloves garlic, minced	2
1	celery stalk, sliced	1
1	carrot, thinly sliced	1
1½ cups	sliced mushrooms	375 mL
2⅓ cups	diced fresh or 1 can	575 mL
	(19 oz/540 mL) diced tomatoes	
⅓ cup	red wine*	75 mL
2 tsp	fresh chopped rosemary	10 mL
2 tsp	fresh chopped basil	10 mL
½ tsp	dried oregano	2 mL
1 tbsp	cornstarch	15 mL
1 tbsp	water	15 mL

Season the pork cubes with salt and pepper to taste. In a large,
heavy-bottomed saucepan, heat the olive oil over medium high heat.
Add the pork, and sauté until browned on all sides. Remove from
the pan and set aside. Add the onion, garlic, celery and carrot to the
pan, and cook until the onions are transparent and soft,
approximately 5 minutes. Add the mushrooms, tomatoes, red wine,
reserved pork, rosemary, basil and oregano. Stir to combine. Cover
and simmer for 15 minutes. In a small dish, dissolve the cornstarch
in the water and stir into the simmering mixture. Continue to
simmer another 5 minutes. Serve hot with rice and your favorite
vegetables.

Red wine can be replaced with beef broth.

Makes 4 servings.

MEDALLIONS OF PORK WITH MAPLE BALSAMIC SAUCE

Sweet cured ham and maple are a traditional combination. Fresh pork and pure maple syrup are equally delicious. The acidic vinegar cuts the maple sweetness a bit, giving a bite to the sauce.

1	large pork tenderloin	1
1 tbsp	olive oil	15 mL
1	clove garlic, minced	1
	Salt to taste	
¼ tsp	freshly ground black pepper	1 mL
2 tbsp	butter	25 mL
½ cup	chopped green onions	125 mL
4 tsp	Dijon mustard	20 mL
2 cups	chicken stock	500 mL
¼ cup	pure maple syrup	50 mL
¼ cup	balsamic vinegar	50 mL
2 tbsp	butter	25 mL

Slice the pork tenderloin crosswise into ½-inch (1-cm) pieces. Place each medallion between two pieces of waxed paper. Put on a flat surface and flatten with a mallet, the side of a meat cleaver or the bottom of a saucepan until ¼ inch (5 mm) thick. In a skillet or fry pan, heat the olive oil and garlic over medium high heat. Add the pork medallions and brown on each side for 3 to 4 minutes. Remove medallions to a warmed serving platter. Season with salt and pepper to taste.

In a saucepan, melt 2 tbsp (25 mL) of butter. Add the green onions and sauté for 30 seconds. Add the Dijon mustard and chicken stock, and reduce over medium heat by one-quarter. Add the maple syrup and balsamic vinegar. Reduce until slightly thickened. Add the remaining butter and stir to thicken. Serve warm over medallions with couscous or rice pilaf.

As an alternative sauce, try the following:

Dijon and Dill Sauce

½ cup	plain yogurt	125 mL
1 tbsp	Dijon mustard	15 mL
1 tbsp	chopped fresh dill or	15 mL
	½ tsp (2 mL) dried	
½ tsp	granulated sugar	2 mL

In the top portion of a double boiler, whisk the yogurt, mustard, dill and sugar until smooth and well combined. Heat over hot, not boiling, water for 2 to 3 minutes or until warm, stirring occasionally to prevent over-heating. This sauce may also be served cold—just whisk ingredients together and serve. Serve warm or cold dill sauce over pork medallions.

Makes 2 to 4 servings.

PORK POT ROAST

Pork available today is lean and marketed as "the other white meat." This is a good roast to serve with any of the root vegetable dishes in the book. But here's an even simpler way to prepare turnip, parsnip and carrot. Peel and cut them into good-sized chunks, coat with olive oil and bake on a flat baking sheet at 375°F (190°C) for 1 hour. The natural sugars in the vegetables caramelize in the baking process and the oil gives a crisp finish.

To help retain the flavor, juiciness and tenderness of pork, don't overcook it. Cook pork until its internal temperature, measured with a meat thermometer, reaches 160°F (70°C).

2 tbsp	vegetable oil	25 mL
2 lbs	shoulder or butt portion of leg	1 kg
1½ cups	unsweetened apple juice	375 mL
1 tsp	salt	5 mL
½ tsp	black pepper	2 mL
2	cinnamon sticks	2
2	medium onions, peeled and sliced	2
1	clove garlic, minced	1
4	medium carrots, peeled and cut into julienne strips	4
1	small rutabaga, peeled and cut into julienne strips	1
2	apples, peeled, cored and diced	2
1 tbsp	freshly squeezed lemon juice	15 mL

In a Dutch oven, heat the oil over medium heat. Add the pork, and cook until browned on all sides. Add the apple juice, salt, pepper, cinnamon sticks, onion and garlic. Bring to a boil and reduce the heat to low. Cover and simmer for 1½ hours. Add the carrots and rutabaga, and simmer for an additional 20 minutes. Prepare the apples and toss them in the lemon juice to prevent browning. Add the apples and cook another 10 minutes.

Makes 6 servings.

CRANBERRY GLAZED PORK LOIN

Fruit glazes seem to complement pork very well. Oranges are often used, but here we maintain the idea of using a tart, acidic fruit by featuring cranberries. The glistening red color gives a lively festive aura to the table.

5 lbs	pork loin roast	2 kg
1 tsp	salt	5 mL
¼ tsp	black pepper	1 mL
½ cup	water	125 mL
3 tbsp	brown sugar	45 mL
3 tbsp	molasses	45 mL
2 tbsp	red wine or cider vinegar	25 mL
4	whole cloves	4
½ tsp	ground cinnamon	2 mL
2 cups	cranberries, fresh or frozen	500 mL

Place the pork loin, fat side up, on a rack in a roasting pan. Rub it all over with the salt and pepper. Roast uncovered in a preheated 350°F (180°C) oven for 2½ hours. Meanwhile, in a medium-sized saucepan, combine the water, brown sugar, molasses, vinegar, cloves and cinnamon. Bring to a boil, then add the cranberries. Reduce the heat and simmer for 10 minutes. Remove the cranberry mixture from the heat and either press through a sieve or process in a food processor fitted with a metal blade, until smooth. Pour the cranberry mixture over the pork roast, increase the oven temperature to 425°F (220°C) and bake for 15 minutes, basting once.

Makes 8 servings.

Scotch Barley Broth

Barley is a favorite grain of the Scottish settlers. This soup is the perfect use for leftover lamb or beef and is so hearty that, with the addition of a freshly baked biscuit or brown bread, it makes a complete meal.

½ cup	dried green peas	125 mL
2 lbs	stewing lamb	1 kg
⅓ cup	pearl barley	75 mL
½ tsp	salt	2 mL
6 cups	water	1.5 L
1	medium onion, chopped	1
2	leeks, chopped	2
3	carrots	3
1	small turnip	1
2	medium potatoes (optional)	2
	Salt and pepper to taste	
1 tbsp	chopped fresh parsley	15 mL

Scotch broth, a thick, hearty broth, is said to be what the Scottish lairds were raised on, accounting for their incredible strength and tenacity.

Soak the dried peas in sufficient water to cover, and leave overnight or 6 to 8 hours. Drain. Dice the meat into bite-sized pieces, removing any excess fat. In a large saucepan or stock pot, combine the meat, peas, barley, salt and water. Over low heat, slowly bring the mixture to the simmering point and simmer for 1½ to 2 hours. Prepare vegetables by cutting into ½-inch (1-cm) cubes. Add diced onion, leeks, carrots, turnip and potatoes to the meat mixture and simmer for an additional 30 minutes, adding more water if required. Adjust seasoning with salt and pepper. Serve hot, garnished with fresh chopped parsley.

Makes 6 to 8 servings.

LAMB SHISH KEBOB

Marinated lamb grilled over glowing coals or under a hot broiler is a succulent meat, slightly charred on the outside but still moist within. Cubed lamb cooks quickly so the meat and the vegetables should be done at the same time. The coriander and cumin give the lamb a Middle Eastern flavor.

½ cup	olive oil	125 mL
⅓ cup	lemon juice	75 mL
1 tsp	salt	5 mL
2¼ tsp	ground coriander	11 mL
¾ tsp	ground cumin	3 mL
1 tsp	chopped fresh oregano	5 mL
1 tsp	ground black pepper	5 mL
¾ cup	finely diced onions	175 mL
4	garlic cloves, chopped	4
2 lbs	boneless lamb shoulder or leg, cut into 1-inch (2.5-cm) cubes	1 kg

In a mixing bowl, whisk the olive oil, lemon juice, salt, coriander, cumin, oregano and pepper until well blended. Stir in the onion and garlic. Put the cubed lamb in a large Ziplock bag or non-metal bowl and pour over the marinade. Toss to coat well. Marinate in the refrigerator for 2 hours. Thread the marinated lamb cubes alternately with your favorite vegetables such as red pepper, zucchini or onions on to metal or soaked wooden skewers. Lightly brush with the marinade and grill or broil for about 10 minutes, turning often to prevent burning, or until the meat is cooked through. Serve with a medley of stir-fried vegetables and rice pilaf.

Makes 4 servings.

ROSEMARY STUFFED LEG OF LAMB

Butchers in most markets will debone a leg of lamb if you ask. This unusual dish uses a thick stuffing of rosemary-scented mashed potatoes to fill the inside of the rolled-up roast. When the leg is roasted and carved, the potato stuffing is set in the center of each slice.

Stuffing

1 tbsp	butter	15 mL
1	large Spanish or sweet onion, finely chopped	1
2 tbsp	chopped fresh rosemary	25 mL
2 tbsp	chopped fresh parsley	25 mL
1 tsp	minced garlic	5 mL
2 cups	warm mashed potatoes	500 mL
1 cup	fine, dry, white bread crumbs	250 mL
3 tbsp	chicken stock	45 mL
	Salt and pepper to taste	
6.5 lbs	leg of lamb, deboned	3 kg
	Salt and pepper to taste	
2 tbsp	lemon juice	25 mL
¼ cup	red wine	50 mL
2 tbsp	port	25 mL
½ cup	black currant jelly	125 mL

Stuffing: In a skillet, melt butter and sauté onion until translucent. Add the rosemary, parsley and garlic, and sauté for 1 minute. In a mixing bowl, blend the warm mashed potatoes and bread crumbs. Add the onion mixture to the potatoes and stir to combine. Add the chicken stock to the mixture. Season with salt and pepper to taste.

Lay the deboned lamb leg on a clean, flat work surface. Open it and season with salt and pepper. Drizzle with fresh lemon juice. Spread stuffing along the center of the open leg and roll to close. Use metal or wooden skewers to hold the roast together during cooking. Place seam side down in a roasting pan. Bake in a preheated 425°F (220°C) oven for 1½ hours for medium rare. Remove the roast, deglaze pan with the red wine and pour off the juices. Remove the fat from the pan juices by adding several ice cubes to congeal the fat. Discard the fat and ice cubes. In a small saucepan, heat the pan juices, port and black currant jelly, stirring until the jelly has dissolved and the sauce is hot.

To serve, slice the meat across the grain, making sure each serving has a generous portion of stuffing in the center of each slice. Pour sauce over the lamb and garnish with a sprig of fresh rosemary. Serve with roasted vegetables and Herbed Potato Sauté (page 96).

Makes 8 to 10 servings.

CHAPTER FIVE

ROOT AND WINTER VEGETABLES

Autumn is glorious in Nova Scotia. The sky is an intense shade of blue not seen at any other time of the year, and the brilliant sun illuminates the leaves turning red and gold. The markets are laden with the end-of-season fruits and vegetables, and the crisp autumn air sparks the appetites for more than the lighter fare of summer. For some, the fall is a sad time. The green leafy vegetables, tomatoes and cucumbers, berries and peaches will soon be gone, replaced by the imports that don't quite measure up in flavor to the home-grown varieties. But this seasonal dilemma needn't be a problem. The cook is still presented with a variety of produce that fits the bill very well.

The fields are bright with ripe orange pumpkins. The other winter squash—acorn, butternut, blue hubbard—are more muted in color and poke out from under massive leaves just beginning to shrink back in the cooler weather. Even more hidden are the potatoes and onions, carrots, parsnips and turnips, which grow underground and need careful harvesting. Altogether these hardy vegetables hold a summer's worth of sun and are deeply flavored. They love long, slow cooking in the soup kettle or stew pot. Finely sliced, their sweetness is released in a quick stir-fry as well. Many chefs have discovered the wonderful technique of slowly roasting the vegetables in large pieces, coated with a little oil. The vegetables' natural sugars caramelize, the outer layers become crisp and the insides are soft and tender.

The early farmers relied greatly on the winter vegetables, since they stored well and were so substantial in texture that they could serve as an extender or substitute for the meat that was scarcer in the coldest winter months. Every farm had a root cellar, which kept a constant cool temperature perfect for long storage. A cool, dry spot is still the best way to store this produce. Basements often have spaces that approximate the root cellar, and can extend the life of a sack of potatoes or some squash.

The pumpkin is the show-off of the winter squashes, brightest in color and capable of growing to a size that seems more appropriate for a boulder than a vegetable. Howard Dill is the internationally renowned pumpkin grower extraordinaire. From his home in the small town of Windsor, Howard has been growing giant pumpkins and distributing their seeds for decades. Now, we really mean giant. Howard's world record pumpkin in 1981 tipped the scales at 493.5 pounds (223.8 kg). Windsor hosts an annual pumpkin festival, which is now one of many sites for an international pumpkin weighoff, offering to the winners cash prizes and great fame in the pumpkin world. Last year's winning pumpkin, accompanied by its grower, traveled to California for a festival there. A rather steep excess baggage charge, we imagine. On a smaller scale, the highly regarded Ross Farm Museum, a historic working farm, opens the spring season with a pumpkin-planting party (say that three times) where children grow their own jack o'lanterns and harvest them in time for Halloween. This wonderful tradition teaches the youngsters something about the growing process and, even better, brings them to the farm several times over the summer to see the changes in farm life as the season progresses.

CARROT SQUARES WITH MAPLE CREAM ICING

These light carrot squares show off the natural sweetness of the carrots. The traditional cream cheese frosting is replaced with a creamy maple-flavored topping.

1 cup	all-purpose white flour	250 mL
1 tsp	baking powder	5 mL
½ tsp	baking soda	2 mL
½ tsp	salt	2 mL
1 tsp	cinnamon	5 mL
½ tsp	ground ginger	2 mL
½ tsp	ground cloves	2 mL
⅔ cup	vegetable oil	150 mL
1 cup	granulated white sugar	250 mL
2	eggs	2
1 cup	grated carrots	250 mL
⅓ cup	chopped walnuts or pecans	75 mL

In a small bowl, combine flour, baking powder, baking soda, salt and spices. In a large bowl, beat together oil and sugar. Beat in eggs, one at a time. Add dry ingredients. Mix well. Fold in carrots and nuts.

Pour batter into greased 8-inch (20-cm) square cake pan. Bake in preheated 350°F (180°C) oven for 50 minutes or until tester inserted in center comes out clean. Cool for 10 minutes. Remove from pan and place on rack to cool. Frost with maple cream icing.

Maple Cream Icing

1	pkg (4 oz/125 g) cream cheese, softened	1
1 tbsp	maple syrup	15 mL
1½ cups	icing sugar	375 mL

In a medium-sized bowl, use a hand beater to mix cream cheese and maple syrup until smooth. Gradually beat in icing sugar.

Makes 16 servings.

BUTTERNUT SQUASH AND CARROT SOUP

Carrots work their magic in this winter squash soup, and the cider vinegar lends a tart accent. Serve this soup piping hot, with the whole-wheat bread recipe that follows.

1	medium butternut squash	1
4	medium carrots	4
1	medium onion, diced	1
2	cloves garlic, minced	2
¼ cup	dry chicken soup base*	50 mL
pinch	salt	pinch
pinch	white pepper	pinch
¼ cup	chopped fresh tarragon	50 mL
¼ cup	cider vinegar	50 mL
¼ cup	butter	50 mL

Peel and coarsely chop the squash and the carrots. Put them in a saucepan. Cover with water and cook until tender crisp. Stir in onion, garlic, dry chicken stock, salt, pepper and fresh tarragon. Simmer for 20 minutes or until the liquid level is even with the vegetables. Strain off cooking liquid through a strainer and return to saucepan. Put cooked vegetables in a food processor and purée until smooth. Stir purée into the cooking liquid. Add cider vinegar and butter. Stir until butter is melted and incorporated into the mixture. Serve hot, garnished with fresh tarragon. This soup can also be served chilled.

Makes 4 to 6 servings.

*Or replace with 10-oz (184-mL) can of chicken broth.

WHOLE-WHEAT BREAD

*One of the simplest yeast breads to make, this one calls
for a combination of whole-wheat and all-purpose flour
that makes a hearty, nutty loaf with a hint of honey.*

3 cups	warm water	750 mL
¾ cup	liquid honey	175 mL
2 tbsp	dry yeast	25 mL
¼ cup	vegetable oil	50 mL
4 cups	whole-wheat flour	1 L
1 tbsp	salt	15 mL
4 to 4½ cups	all-purpose flour	1 L to 1.125 L

In a large mixing bowl, mix the water and honey until the honey is
dissolved. Stir in the yeast. Let rest for 5 minutes. Stir in the oil, followed by 4 cups (1 L) of the whole-wheat flour and the salt. Beat
until smooth. Add the all-purpose flour 1 cup (250 mL) at a time
until a stiff dough is formed and dough comes away clean from the
sides. Turn the dough onto a floured surface and knead until the
dough is smooth and elastic. Place it in an oiled bowl. Cover it and
let rise in a warm place until double in size, about 1 hour. Punch
down and let rise until double in size again for another hour. Punch
the dough down again and divide into two. Form a loaf from each
piece and place in a greased 9 x 5 inch (23 x 12 cm) loaf pan. Let
rise again until dough is slightly above the edge of the pan. Bake for
1 hour in a preheated 350°F (180°C) oven.

Makes 2 loaves.

HERBED POTATO SAUTÉ

A simple aromatic combination of potatoes and herbs.
The oil and butter combination is a trick that keeps the
fat from burning at the hot temperature needed to devel-
op the beautiful brown crust.

4	medium potatoes	4
3 cups	chicken stock or salted water	750 mL
1 tbsp	butter	15 mL
1 tbsp	olive oil	15 mL
2 tsp	fresh rosemary, finely chopped	10 mL

Scrub potatoes (or peel if desired) and cut into 1-inch (2.5-cm) pieces. In a saucepan, bring potatoes and chicken stock or water to a boil. Cook until tender but still firm. Drain and allow to cool completely. Heat the butter and olive oil in a large skillet over medium heat. Add the potatoes and rosemary, and sauté about 10 minutes, stirring occasionally to prevent burning. Serve hot.

Makes 4 servings.

TANGY POTATO SALAD

*A version of this potato salad surely has appeared
at countless picnics and church suppers. Served with
lobster, baked ham or fresh fish, it is the ultimate salad
for informal outdoor dining.*

6	medium potatoes, cooked and diced	6
1	medium carrot, grated	1
1	medium apple, peeled and diced	1
2	hard-boiled eggs, chopped	2
½ cup	green relish or chopped pickles	125 mL
1	stalk celery, diced	1
¼ cup	Italian dressing	50 mL
1 cup	mayonnaise or salad dressing	250 mL
1 tsp	salt	5 mL
½ tsp	black pepper	2 mL
2 tbsp	chopped parsley	25 mL

In a large bowl, combine potatoes, carrot, apple, eggs, relish and
celery. In a small bowl, whisk Italian dressing, mayonnaise, salt and
pepper until well blended. Pour dressing over potato mixture, and
mix well. Cover and refrigerate for several hours before serving, stirring occasionally. Garnish with parsley.

Makes 6 servings.

KOHL CANNON

Cabbage is a winter vegetable that grows so well it makes any gardener look like a pro. It displays a range of flavor and texture, depending upon the method of preparation. Consider how different the piquant cabbage-based sauerkraut is from the silky, buttery braised cabbage or a crunchy stir-fry.

Lunenburg, our historic ship-building center, is also the center for the German immigrants who have been in Nova Scotia since the 1800s. Kohl Cannon, or Colcannon, combines the easily stored cabbage, turnips and potatoes in a simple, hearty mixture.

1	head cabbage	1
5	slices of turnip	5
5	medium-sized potatoes	5
¼ lb	butter	125 g
	Salt and pepper to taste	

Cook cabbage and turnip just until crisp. Add potatoes and cook all together until potatoes are tender. Drain and add butter, salt and pepper. Mash.

Makes 6 to 8 servings.

CHEESY POTATO-VEGETABLE SOUP

Thick and very satisfying, this potato and vegetable soup is a meal in itself with the addition of cheddar cheese. It would be perfect with the potato bannock that follows.

¼ cup	butter or vegetable oil	50 mL
1	clove garlic, minced	1
1	large onion, chopped	1
2 cups	cubed potatoes	500 mL
1	large carrot, diced	1
2 tsp	salt	10 mL
½ tsp	dried sweet basil	2 mL
½ tsp	celery seed	2 mL
4 cups	chopped broccoli or cauliflower or combination of the two	1 L
3 cups	water	750 mL
1 cup	milk	250 mL
1 cup	grated cheddar cheese	250 mL

In a large saucepan or pot, melt butter. Add garlic, onion, potatoes, carrot, salt, basil and celery seed. Sauté for 5 minutes. Add broccoli and/or cauliflower. Sauté an additional minute. Add water and bring to a boil. Reduce heat and simmer, covered, until the vegetables are tender. Transfer vegetables to a food processor and purée, leaving some chunks. Transfer back to the saucepan, and stir in the milk and cheese. Adjust seasonings with salt and pepper. Heat until the cheese is melted and the soup is hot. Garnish with fresh chopped chives.

Makes 6 servings.

POTATO BANNOCK

Bannock is a traditional bread that has transcended not only generations but also cultures. We think the Irish had their hand in this version, with the addition of mashed potatoes to the dough. The potatoes lighten the dough, adding moisture.

2⅓ cups	all-purpose flour	575 mL
1 tsp	salt	5 mL
2 tbsp	baking powder	25 mL
¼ cup	granulated sugar	50 mL
2 tbsp	vegetable shortening	25 mL
¾ cup	cooked and mashed potatoes	175 mL
1 cup	water	250 mL

In a mixing bowl, combine flour, salt, baking powder and sugar. Cut in shortening with a fork or pastry blender to form a coarse crumb. Stir in potatoes and water until blended. Turn dough out on a lightly floured board and knead gently 10 times, adding extra flour to dough until it no longer sticks to your hands. Place dough on an ungreased baking sheet and pat out with hands until 1 inch (2.5 cm) thick. Bake in a preheated 450°F (230°C) oven for 18 to 20 minutes.

Cut into pieces and serve hot or cold.

Makes 8 to 10 pieces.

HERBED POTATO PUFF

Easier to make than a soufflé and low in calories, the potato puff is an out-of-the-ordinary side dish. Use freshly mashed potatoes.

2	eggs, separated	2
2 cups	hot mashed potatoes	500 mL
½ cup	skim milk	125 mL
¼ cup	plain yogurt	125 mL
1 tsp	salt	5 mL
¼ tsp	freshly ground black pepper	1 mL
1	clove garlic, minced	1
1 tsp	dried sweet basil	5 mL
2	chopped green onions including green stalk	2
2 tbsp	fresh chopped parsley	25 mL
½ cup	grated mozzarella cheese	125 mL

In a mixing bowl, beat the egg whites until stiff peaks form. Place the egg yolks, mashed potatoes, milk, yogurt, salt, pepper, garlic and basil in a food processor and process until well blended and smooth. Transfer potato mixture to a bowl and stir in green onions, parsley and cheese. Fold in beaten egg white. Place in a well-greased 2-quart (2-L) casserole dish and bake, uncovered, in a pre-heated 350°F (180°C) oven for 30 to 40 minutes or until the center is set.

Makes 6 servings.

SCALLOPED POTATOES AND PARSNIPS

Here is a variation on traditional scalloped potatoes. Parsnips, which taste like nutty carrots, bake into tender slices. Be sure to use small parsnips, because larger parsnips need long cooking in liquid or they will have a woody texture.

2	small parsnips	2
2	medium potatoes	2
	Salt and freshly ground black pepper to taste	
1 cup	milk (low fat is fine)	250 mL
½ cup	chicken broth or stock	125 mL
4½ tsp	all-purpose flour	22 mL
1	large onion	1
1 tbsp	vegetable oil	15 mL

Peel the parsnips and potatoes and slice into ⅛-inch (3-mm) slices. Mix together in a bowl, tossing with the salt and pepper. In a mixing bowl, whisk the milk, chicken broth and flour until smooth. Peel and dice onion into ½-inch (1-cm) pieces. Heat the oil in a large saucepan and sauté the onions over medium heat until just soft. Add the potato/parsnip mixture, followed by the milk mixture, stirring to combine. Bring mixture back to a simmer and simmer for 1 minute, stirring often.

Grease an 8-inch (20-cm) square baking pan with butter or vegetable spray, and add the potato mixture. Bake in a preheated 425°F (220°C) oven for 45 minutes or until the top is golden brown and the vegetables are tender.

Makes 4 servings.

PARSNIP AND APPLE SOUP

Another wonderful combination of fall fruits and root vegetables. Sage is often reserved for poultry stuffing, which is too bad since its unique flavor is a great accent. Fresh sage is best here, but use dried if fresh is unavailable.

1 lb	parsnips	500 g
1	large cooking apple	1
2 tbsp	butter	25 mL
3 cups	chicken stock	750 mL
4	fresh sage leaves	4
	or ¼ tsp (1 mL) dried	
2	whole cloves	2
1 cup	light cream (18%)	250 mL
	Salt and pepper to taste	

Peel and coarsely chop the parsnips and apple. In a large saucepan, melt the butter. Add the parsnips and apple, and cook, covered, for 10 minutes, stirring occasionally. Add stock, sage and cloves. Bring to a boil. Reduce heat. Cover and simmer for 30 minutes or until the parsnips are soft. Remove the sage leaves and cloves. Transfer the parsnip/apple mixture to a food processor or blender and purée until smooth. Return to saucepan, stir in cream and season to taste with salt and pepper. Reheat but do not allow to boil. Serve hot. Garnish with fresh sage or parsley and croutons.

Makes 4 to 6 servings.

Parsnips are a wonderful vegetable for soups and stews. Tasting slightly like a carrot (to which it is related and which it resembles in shape), the parsnip needs to be cooked before eating. Since they actually improve in flavor after a frost, they are best in the wintertime. Puréed and mixed with puréed pear, sautéed first in butter, parsnips make an elegant dish perfect with roasted chicken or pork. Try peeling, boiling and mashing them like potatoes as well.

BAKED TURNIPS AND APPLES

Many think of the turnip only as the large winter vegetable used in stews. While this is a great use for the easy-to-grow and easy-to-store turnip, the small early-harvested roots found in the early fall are delicious and sweet when washed, trimmed and steamed. There is consistent confusion about the difference between turnips and rutabagas, which are a different species. The large yellow variety of both vegetables do look similar and can be used interchangeably. Try glazing the turnip with some maple syrup for a real treat.

Again we pair apples with a root vegetable, in this case the often-ignored turnip. The ingredients are reminiscent of a dessert crisp, but there is no mistaking the flavor of the turnip.

1	large turnip	1
1 tbsp	butter	15 mL
1 cup	milk	250 mL
3 tbsp	brown sugar	45 mL
½ tsp	ground cinnamon	2 mL
1½ cups	sliced and peeled apples	375 mL
¼ cup	all-purpose flour	50 mL
¼ cup	brown sugar	50 mL
2 tbsp	butter	25 mL

Peel and chop turnip. Cook turnip in water until tender. Drain. Add the butter and milk, and mash. In a mixing bowl, combine sugar and cinnamon. Add apples and toss to coat. Grease a 6-cup (1.5-L) casserole dish. Starting and ending with the turnip, arrange alternate layers of turnip and apples. In a small bowl, combine flour and brown sugar. Cut butter in to make a fine crumb and sprinkle over the top of the casserole.

Bake in a preheated 350°F (180°C) oven for 1 hour. Serve hot.

Makes 8 servings.

GINGER PEAR BEETS

The cubed ruby-red beets mixed in with the spicy-sweet pear purée are bright and beautiful. This fruit and vegetable combination is perfectly balanced.

5	beets	5
3	ripe pears	3
2 tbsp	lemon juice	25 mL
1 tsp	cornstarch	5 mL
1 tbsp	liquid honey	15 mL
1 tsp	grated fresh ginger root	5 mL
	or ¼ tsp (1 mL) ground ginger	
¼ tsp	salt	1 mL

Wash beets and trim, leaving on 1 inch (2.5 cm) of the stem and root. In a saucepan, cover beets with sufficient water to cover and bring to a boil over medium high heat. Reduce heat and cook until beets are tender, about 25 minutes. Drain. In a dish of cold water, rub the beet skins with your fingers and they will easily peel off. Cool. Dice into ½-inch (1-cm) pieces.

Peel and seed pears, then cut into pieces. Put pears and lemon juice in a food processor and process until smooth. Put puréed pears and cornstarch in a medium-sized saucepan. Stir in honey, ginger root and salt. Bring to a boil over medium heat, stirring constantly, and allow to boil for approximately 1 minute until thickened. Reduce heat. Add the beets to the pear mixture. Heat until beets have warmed.

Makes 4 servings.

Most commonly found in the market is the deep red beet that is essential for the Eastern European–influenced soup called "borscht." Today we can also find golden and red-and-white-striped Chioggia beets that make a beautiful composed salad. Don't discard the crunchy beet greens (the leafy tops) if they are attached. Trimmed and well washed, the greens steam into a delicious side dish. For those with English cookbooks, beets are called "beetroots."

CABBAGE WITH TANGY MUSTARD SAUCE

In our last book, we combined beets with mustard. Now we bring the same technique to cabbage. The sauce is clingy and thick, and the cooked cabbage loses the some-what bitter taste many associate with the vegetable.

1	medium-sized cabbage	1
¼ cup	melted butter	50 mL
¼ cup	all-purpose flour	50 mL
1½ cups	chicken stock	375 mL
2	slices bacon, fried crisp	2
¾ tsp	Dijon mustard	3 mL
1 tbsp	freshly squeezed lemon juice	15 mL
	Dash of nutmeg	
2 tsp	grated carrot	10 mL
2 tsp	minced fresh parsley	10 mL
1 tbsp	dry white wine	15 mL
¼ cup	heavy or whipping cream (35%)	50 mL
	Salt and pepper to taste	

Cut cabbage into 6 pieces. Place them in a saucepan and boil until tender. Remove from heat, drain and set aside.

In a small saucepan over medium heat, melt butter. Add flour, whisking for 1 to 2 minutes until well blended and cooked. Gradually add chicken stock, whisking constantly until sauce thickens. Reduce heat to low. Dice bacon, and add to sauce. Add mustard, lemon juice, nutmeg, carrot, parsley and wine. Stir to combine. Increase heat to medium and add whipping cream. Continue stirring and cook for an additional 5 minutes. Adjust seasonings.

Put cabbage in a serving dish, and pour hot sauce over it. Garnish with fresh chopped parsley and a sprinkle of nutmeg.

Makes 6 servings.

PUMPKIN BREAD

This reddish-brown sweet and chewy quick bread is easy to make and gives a new use for pumpkin. One trick is to have all the ingredients out and ready before beginning the mixing process. This recipe makes two loaves, one for now and one for the freezer.

4	eggs	4
2 cups	granulated sugar	500 mL
1¼ cups	vegetable oil	300 mL
2 cups	puréed pumpkin	500 mL
3 cups	all-purpose flour	750 mL
2 tsp	baking soda	10 mL
2 tsp	baking powder	10 mL
1 tsp	salt	5 mL
1 tbsp	ground cinnamon	15 mL
1½ cups	raisins (optional)	375 mL

In a large mixing bowl, whisk the eggs until well beaten. Add the sugar, oil and puréed pumpkin and whisk until well blended. In a separate bowl, blend the flour, baking soda and powder, salt and cinnamon. Stir into pumpkin mixture until well combined. Fold in raisins. Pour batter into two greased 8 x 4 inch (20 x 10 cm) loaf pans. Bake in a preheated 350°F (180°C) oven for 1 hour or until tester inserted in the center comes out clean. Remove from oven. Cool in pan for 10 minutes, and then carefully turn out onto a wire rack to finish cooling.

Makes 2 loaves.

Record books abound with Nova Scotia–grown championship pumpkins weighing in at more than 700 lbs (300 kg). Such sumo vegetables offer little to the cook, since their flavor and texture would be akin to that of the maple tree. Happily, we also grow smaller varieties such as the 1 to 2 lb (450 to 900 g) sugar pumpkin. Baked for an hour in a 350°F (180°C) oven after the top, the seeds and the stringy fibers have been removed, a deeply flavored dish emerges.

CHAPTER SIX

FROM THE VINE AND THE BUSH

In the early days, when Nova Scotia was being settled by the Europeans, families did not have specialized occupations. They lived by the shore, had some land and grew their own vegetables. That made them farmers. When winter covered the land with snow, they left the fields and took their food from the sea. They were fishermen then. Over the years, some folks stayed near the coast and supplied fish for their own tables and their neighbors', and others moved inland to the more fertile, warmer valleys and brought their vegetables to the provincial markets. Despite the prevailing notion that the family farm is in decline, in Nova Scotia we are seeing a resurgence of interest in farming among younger people, some of them two generations removed from working the soil. We have a growing organic farming movement, dedicated to using natural techniques, including digging in organic matter, planting complementary crops for insect and disease control, and rotating the crops in the fields. In addition, green houses and an emerging hydroponics industry (growing plants in water rather than soil) are increasing the kinds of produce we can cultivate and extending our short growing season. In the summer and fall, the farmers' markets teem with local produce of all kinds. Even warm-climate crops like cantaloupe and watermelon can be found in years when mother nature holds off the first frost until late September or so. And when that does not happen, we have our share of green tomato chutney and relish as well.

The rebirth of the family farm is good news for the chefs and cooks of Nova Scotia. The variety of produce is expanding under the care of a younger generation of farmers. In the early 1980s Moh and Judith Hardin decided that Nova Scotia restaurants and markets would buy a wide selection of locally grown fresh herbs, and Riverview Farm, in Maitland, started growing basil, oregano, marjoram, thyme, chives, dill, mint and more—and not just one type of any given herb, but beautiful varieties with subtle differences in taste. Their sense of the market was accurate, and now fresh herbs are delivered from farms around the province. The current owners of the farm host a provincial herb festival each summer. A favorite herb is summer savory, grown by many farmers and found in virtually every supermarket in Nova Scotia. Although this herb is unfamiliar to most North Americans, Europeans consider it to be the best seasoning for beans, and we also use it in herbed biscuits. Some farmers are adding edible "weeds" to their crop list, so that now dandelion greens and lamb's quarters can be found, freshly picked, cleaned and ready for the salad bowl.

Watch for fresh, local produce as it comes in season. From the first fiddleheads and asparagus in the spring to the abundant tomatoes, cucumbers, corn and green beans through the summer, any vegetable will be at the peak of its flavor soon after it has been picked. Play with the wide variety of color, texture and shapes of the vegetables available today, and try a vegetarian menu from time to time. It will stretch your creativity. Our chefs and cooks are working with unusual combinations of vegetables, herbs and spices to complement the seafood, meat and poultry that is still the focus of most menus. Drive almost anywhere in Nova Scotia and, once you get a bit off the main road, it is likely that you will find a family farm, perhaps with a barnboard-sided stand at the end of the driveway with some fresh-picked vegetables and perhaps a bottle of herb-flavored oil or vinegar, a jug of apple cider or some fresh biscuits for sale. More and more often, the supermarket produce section will feature items labeled "locally grown." The family farm is coming back, if indeed it ever went away, and the city dweller should be very grateful.

FRESH TOMATO SOUP

Regardless of the variety, tomatoes ripened on the vine and brought to market in season offer the most remarkable flavor of the summer. (Ripening a summer tomato just turning red from orange in the kitchen also works well.) During the rest of the year, we can find varieties of greenhouse-grown tomatoes or those "vine-ripened" from the south. Try using a good-quality canned tomato and tomato paste for winter dishes that need the tomato taste. Reconstituted sun-dried tomatoes offer another alternative.

For those who equate tomato soup with the creamy pink canned variety, here is an eye-opener. This soup is as tasty as it is versatile—it is a great way of using an over-abundance of fresh tomatoes. (In a pinch, canned whole or diced tomatoes can be successfully substituted.) As for the fresh herbs, fresh dill and oregano can be used instead of basil and thyme. Garnish with a snip of fresh dill and a dollop of sour cream.

3 cups	peeled, chopped tomatoes	750 mL
2 cups	water or chicken stock	500 mL
½ cup	diced onion	125 mL
1	clove garlic, minced	1
1	5½-oz (156-mL) can of tomato paste	1
1 tsp	salt	5 mL
¼ cup	chopped fresh parsley	50 mL
¼ cup	chopped fresh basil	50 mL
1 tbsp	chopped fresh thyme	15 mL
1 cup	milk	250 mL
	Freshly ground black pepper to taste	

In a saucepan, combine tomatoes, water or chicken stock, onion and garlic and simmer, covered, for 15 minutes. Add tomato paste and salt. Put in a food processor or blender and blend until smooth. Return to saucepan and stir in fresh herbs, milk and pepper. This soup may be served hot, or refrigerated, covered, and served cold. Garnish with fresh herbs.

Makes 6 servings.

BRUSCHETTA

*Juicy vine-ripened tomatoes on chewy bread make a
summery starter course or a light snack.*

1 cup	diced fresh tomatoes, skinned and seeded*	250 mL
½ cup	grated mozzarella cheese	125 mL
1 tbsp	grated Parmesan cheese	15 mL
¼ cup	extra-virgin olive oil	50 mL
1 tbsp	finely chopped fresh garlic	25 mL
1 tbsp	finely chopped fresh basil or 1 tsp (5 mL) dried	25 mL
2 tsp	chopped fresh parsley Freshly ground black pepper to taste Salt to taste	10 mL

In a mixing bowl, stir together all the ingredients until well blended.

To serve, spread on top of French bread, foccacia bread or pizza
dough. Sprinkle with additional Parmesan cheese, if desired. Bake
in a preheated 400°F (200°C) oven until cheeses have melted. If
using pizza dough, cook until dough is done.

**1 cup (250 mL) canned diced tomatoes, drained, may be
substituted.*

Makes 1½ cups (375 mL) of topping.

FRIED GREEN TOMATOES

Fried green tomatoes—our simple answer to the dilemma that faces every home gardener in our climate: What to do with the inevitable crop of tomatoes that didn't ripen before the weather turned cool. Use fried green tomatoes as a side dish or serve at breakfast.

6	small green tomatoes	6
3 tbsp	all-purpose flour	45 mL
1 tsp	granulated sugar	5 mL
1 tsp	salt	5 mL
	Pepper to taste	
¼ cup	chopped raw bacon	50 mL

Wash tomatoes and cut in ½-inch (1-cm) slices. In a shallow dish, mix together flour, sugar, salt and pepper. Coat tomato slices with flour mixture, one slice at a time. In a heavy frying pan or skillet over medium heat, cook the chopped bacon until crisp. Add tomato slices and brown on both sides. Serve hot.

Makes 6 servings.

SPINACH SOUP

A two-in-one recipe. You can stop after sautéeing the spinach and use the results as a side dish vegetable or continue the recipe and create a delightful green soup that makes an appetizer course for seafood or poultry.

8 oz	fresh spinach	250 g
2 tbsp	butter	25 mL
1 cup	finely chopped Spanish onion	250 mL
1½ tsp	minced garlic	7 mL
1 tsp	dried tarragon	5 mL
2 cups	heavy or whipping cream (35%)	500 mL
1½ tsp	dried chicken stock*	7 mL
½ cup	water	125 mL

Wash spinach and remove stems. In a saucepan over medium heat, melt the butter and sauté the onions and garlic until onions are tender crisp. Do not brown. Add spinach to onions and garlic and sauté until limp. This may be used as a vegetable at this point.

To continue on and make a soup: Add dried tarragon. Cool. When cool, put spinach mixture in a food processor and purée. Return purée to the saucepan and add the whipping cream. Dissolve the chicken stock base in the water and add to the spinach mixture. Heat to boiling, then reduce to a simmer. This soup is better made the day ahead and may be served hot or cold. Garnish with a small fresh spinach leaf, tarragon sprig or watercress.

Makes 6 servings.

*Or ½ cup (125 mL) canned chicken broth.

Because it does best in cool weather and is fast growing, markets carry beautiful dark green spinach at the beginning and the end of the season. Be sure the spinach is well washed and free from sand. Large leaves can be removed from the thick stem before cooking; small leaves can be used whole. Remove any spotted or wilted leaves before using the spinach. They will ruin the dish.

HERBED BISCUITS

Herbed biscuits are a tasty delight that can be made in short order. The herb-flecked dough and the savory flavor are perfect with a simply seasoned chowder or soup.

2 cups	all-purpose flour	500 mL
4 tsp	baking powder	20 mL
½ tsp	salt	2 mL
1 tsp	granulated sugar	5 mL
⅛ tsp	paprika	0.5 mL
½ tsp	dried rosemary	2 mL
½ tsp	dried thyme	2 mL
½ tsp	dried sage	2 mL
¼ cup	butter, softened	50 mL
1 cup	milk	250 mL

In a mixing bowl, combine flour, baking powder, salt and sugar. Stir in herbs and spices. Add butter and cut into flour mixture with a fork or pastry blender, until it resembles a coarse crumb. Add the milk and stir gently, taking care not to overmix as biscuits will be tough. Turn dough out onto a lightly floured board and quickly knead 5 or 6 times. Roll out dough to ½ inch (1 cm) thick and use a floured biscuit cutter or glass to cut out biscuits. Place on an ungreased baking pan and bake in a preheated 400°F (200°C) oven for 15 to 17 minutes.

Makes 18 biscuits.

SPINACH SALAD WITH CREAMY DRESSING

This spinach salad has a light, smooth dressing. The plain yogurt and lemon juice provide a tang.

Dressing

½ cup	plain yogurt	125 mL
½ cup	milk	125 mL
⅓ cup	lemon juice	75 mL
1 tbsp	liquid honey	15 mL
1 tbsp	finely chopped fresh chives	15 mL
	Salt and paprika to taste	

Salad

8 oz	fresh spinach	250 g
6	slices of bacon, fried and crumbled	6
4	eggs, hard-boiled and sliced	4
1 cup	sliced mushrooms	250 mL
1 cup	grated mozzarella cheese	250 mL

Dressing: In a food processor or blender, process the yogurt, milk, lemon juice and honey until well blended and smooth. Add the chives, and season to taste with salt and paprika. Place in a covered container and chill until serving time to blend flavors.

Salad: Wash, dry and tear spinach leaves into bite-sized pieces. In a large salad bowl, layer ingredients beginning with the spinach followed by the bacon, egg slices, mushrooms and cheese.

Just before serving, pour dressing over salad and toss.

Makes 6 servings.

ROASTED PURÉE OF CARROT AND ZUCCHINI SOUP

The carrots and a hint of curry create a sweet base for this soup. Its deep flavor is even more enhanced by the unusual step of roasting the vegetables before adding them to the stock and cream.

2	large carrots	2
1	medium onion	1
2	medium zucchini	2
2 tbsp	olive oil	25 mL
4	cloves garlic, chopped	4
1 tsp	curry powder	5 mL
	Salt and pepper to taste	
4 cups	chicken stock	1 L
½ cup	heavy or whipping cream (35%)	125 mL

Peel the carrots and onion and dice into ¾-inch (2-cm) squares. Wash and trim ends of the zucchini and cut into ¾-inch (2-cm) squares. In a Dutch oven, heat the olive oil and sauté the carrots, onion and zucchini for 7 minutes. Add the garlic, curry, salt and pepper and stir to combine. Cover and roast in a preheated 375°F (180°C) oven for 15 minutes. Remove from oven. Add the chicken stock and cook over medium heat for 7 minutes. Add the cream, adjust seasonings and transfer to a food processor or blender and purée until smooth. Serve hot. Garnish with whipping cream and fresh chervil.

Makes 4 to 6 servings.

HERBED GREEN BEANS

Lemon and rosemary season the green beans to make a bright side dish that is excellent with fish.

4 cups	fresh green beans	1 L
¼ cup	butter	50 mL
⅔ cup	chopped onion	150 mL
1	clove of garlic, minced	1
¼ cup	diced celery	50 mL
¼ cup	chopped fresh parsley or 1 tsp (15 mL) dried	50 mL
1 tbsp	lemon juice	15 mL
¼ tsp	rosemary	1 mL
½ tsp	salt	2 mL
	Pepper to taste	

Fresh beans are usually sold in their pods and include green beans. The old recipes call them "string beans," but new varieties abound that have little or none of the inedible fiber.

Wash and trim ends of beans and cut into 2-inch (5-cm) pieces. In a saucepan, boil sufficient water to cover prepared beans, add beans and bring water back to a boil. Reduce heat and cook until desired doneness is reached. Remove from heat, drain and reserve liquid.

In a small saucepan, melt butter and sauté onions, garlic and celery until onion is transparent. Add remaining ingredients. Stir to combine and simmer for 4 minutes, stirring occasionally. Add to green beans, and toss well to coat.

Makes 6 servings.

MRS. WEBSTER'S BAKED BEANS

A mainstay of the cold-weather diet, these have great flavor and nutritional value. The key to success in cooking with dried beans is to soak them long enough. It does not hurt to start the soaking the day before you plan to use them. Many people use an alternative soaking method, bringing the beans and sufficient water to cover to a boil for 5 minutes in a covered saucepan. They then remove the beans from the heat and let stand. They can be used a couple of hours later. This method works in a pinch, but we prefer the long soak.

If baked beans and brown bread are on the table, it must be Saturday night in the Maritimes! This Saturday night tradition is something many Nova Scotians grew up on. Baked beans also show up at countless church suppers and community gatherings. The key to successful baked beans is the parboiling of the beans and the long, slow baking with enough liquid to keep the dish moist.

1 lb	baking beans	454 g
2 tsp	dried mustard	10 mL
½ cup	brown sugar	125 mL
⅔ cup	molasses	150 mL
1 tsp	salt	5 mL
¼ tsp	black pepper	1 mL
3 oz	salt pork or bacon, coarsely chopped	90 g
1 tsp	white vinegar	5 mL
1 cup	water	250 mL
1	medium onion, quartered	1

1/2 cup Ketchup

In a large bowl, cover beans with plenty of water, and soak overnight; or put beans in a large saucepan with 6 cups (1.5 L) of water and boil for 5 minutes, covered. Remove from heat and let stand for 1 hour. Drain and rinse beans.

In a large saucepan, add beans to 6 cups (1.5 L) of water. Bring to a boil and boil, covered, for 5 minutes. Reduce heat and simmer until beans are tender, approximately 1 hour. Test doneness by taking a bean from the pot and blowing on it. If the skin of the bean cracks, they are ready. If simmered too long, the beans will become mushy; not long enough will make them hard. Drain and rinse them and place in a slow cooker or bean crock (a roaster also works).

In a small bowl, mix together the dried mustard, sugar, molasses, salt, pepper, salt pork or bacon, vinegar and water. Pour over beans.

Stir gently. Add enough water to cover the beans. Top with quartered onion.

If cooking in a slow cooker, cook on high for 4 to 6 hours, or bake, covered, in a preheated 300°F (150°C) oven for 4 to 6 hours. Add water during the cooking process if necessary. Avoid excess stirring.

Serve hot with brown bread.

Makes 6 cups (1.5 L).

ZUCCHINI BREAD

Zucchini is easy to grow, and the large leaves serve to hide the zucchini, which ought to be picked when 6 to 8 inches (15 to 20 cm) long. The immense, baseball bat–like product is good for compost, being much too tough and poorly flavored to eat. The smaller zucchini is sweet and crisp. It is one "summer" vegetable that can successfully be purchased year round, with little sacrifice of flavor. The English refer to them as "vegetable marrows."

The unwritten law of the home gardener is that no matter how few zucchini seeds are planted, the resulting crop will be far more than a family will or can consume. This no doubt accounts for the number of creative recipes that contain zucchini. Zucchini bread makes a good tea snack and freezes well for later use.

2 cups	finely chopped zucchini	500 mL
3	eggs	3
2¼ cups	granulated sugar	550 mL
1 cup	vegetable oil	250 mL
2 tsp	vanilla	10 mL
3 cups	all-purpose flour	750 mL
1 tsp	salt	5 mL
1 tsp	baking soda	5 mL
¼ tsp	baking powder	1 mL
1 tbsp	ground cinnamon	15 mL
1 cup	raisins or nuts (optional)	250 mL

Peel and seed zucchini. Either chop finely with a sharp knife or process in a food processor. Set pulp aside.

In a large mixing bowl, using an electric hand mixer, beat together the eggs and sugar. Gradually beat in the oil. Add the vanilla. In a mixing bowl, blend the flour, salt, baking soda and powder and cinnamon. Beat or stir flour mixture into egg mixture, followed by the zucchini and raisins and/or nuts. Pour into two greased 8 x 4 inch (20 x 10 cm) loaf pans. Bake in a preheated 350°F (180°C) oven for 45 minutes or until tester inserted in the center comes out clean. Remove from oven. Allow to cool in pans for 5 minutes and then turn out on to wire racks.

Makes 2 loaves.

DRESSED-UP PEAS

Make this dish with snow peas or fresh shelled sweet peas. Either way, the interesting combination of mint and curry coats the sweet peas. The grated carrot adds some texture and its color sets off the green peas.

2 cups	snow peas	500 mL
2 tbsp	butter or margarine	25 mL
¼ cup	chopped onions	50 mL
1 cup	sliced mushrooms	250 mL
½ tsp	salt	2 mL
¼ tsp	curry powder	1 mL
¼ cup	mint jelly	50 mL
2 tbsp	grated carrot	25 mL

Wash and trim ends of snow peas. In a medium-sized saucepan, melt butter over medium heat. Add onions and mushrooms and sauté until onions are transparent. Add salt, curry powder and mint jelly, stirring until jelly has dissolved. Add peas and grated carrot and sauté until peas are tender crisp. Serve at once.

Makes 4 to 6 servings.

Brown Bread

Molasses is the old-fashioned ingredient that gives the brown color and sweetness to this easy-to-make bread, which is the traditional bread served with baked beans. Cut into 1-inch (2.5-cm) thick slices, toast it and serve it with a pure fruit preserve.

3 cups	boiling water	750 mL
1½ cups	rolled oats	375 mL
1 tbsp	salt	15 mL
3 tbsp	brown sugar	45 mL
⅓ cup	butter	75 mL
1¼ cups	molasses	300 mL
1 tbsp	granulated sugar	15 mL
1½ cups	warm water	375 mL
2 tbsp	dry yeast	25 mL
11–12 cups	all-purpose flour	2.75–3 L

In a large bowl, stir rolled oats, salt, brown sugar, butter and molasses into the boiling water. Set aside to cool. In a small mixing bowl, dissolve the sugar in warm water, add yeast and set aside to let rise until foamy. Add yeast mixture to cooled oatmeal mixture and stir to combine. Stir in flour 1 cup (250 mL) at a time until dough comes away clean from the sides of the bowl. Turn dough out onto a lightly floured surface and knead until smooth and elastic. Place in a greased bowl, cover and let rise for approximately 1½ hours or until double in bulk. Punch down and divide dough into 4 pieces. Form four loaves and place in greased 9 x 5 inch (23 x 12 cm) loaf pans. Cover and let rise for 1¼ hours or until double in size. Bake in a preheated 350°F (180°C) oven for 35 to 40 minutes. Remove from pans and allow to cool.

Makes 4 loaves.

ASPARAGUS AND LEEK SOUP

A perfect luncheon soup or a great lead-in to a seafood entrée. It's not quite a cream soup—we keep some of the whole pieces of leek and asparagus to add texture and color to the creamy base. Take care not to overcook the asparagus.

3	leeks	3
2 tbsp	butter	25 mL
1	clove garlic, minced	1
1 tsp	minced fresh dill or	5 mL
	⅛ tsp (0.5 mL) dried	
1 lb	asparagus	500 g
1¾ cups	chicken stock or broth	425 mL
½ cup	water	125 mL
½ cup	sour cream, regular or light	125 mL
	Salt and ground black pepper to taste	

Trim and discard the dark green portion of the leek. Wash them very well and chop. In a saucepan, melt the butter and add the garlic, dill and leeks. Sauté until leeks are tender, but not browned.

Trim the tough ends from the asparagus and cut into 1-inch (2.5-cm) pieces. Add the asparagus, chicken stock and water. Cover and simmer for 10 minutes or until the asparagus is tender.

Transfer two-thirds of the mixture to a food processor and process until smooth. Return puréed mixture to the remaining ingredients in the saucepan and stir to blend. Add the sour cream and whisk until well blended. Season with salt and pepper and reheat to serve.

Makes 4 servings.

In choosing asparagus look for bright green stalks and tips that are tight and firm. While peeling the thicker stalks is one approach, the more common style is to snap the stalk to break off the tough part. This is a vegetable that needs quick cooking and should be served while still a little crisp. We have found that the microwave does a great job. Set the stalks in a large-enough bowl or pan, add about ½ cup (125 mL) of water and ¼ teaspoon (1 mL) of salt for 12 stalks, cover and cook about five minutes (more or less, depending upon your microwave).

VEGETABLE STRATA

Vegetable strata, with its layers of colorful vegetables, is an eye-appealing and nutritious vegetarian dish that can be the centerpiece of a lunch or light dinner. Make variations to the vegetables recommended in the recipe as long as you cut them in similar sizes so that they will cook evenly.

1½ cups	sliced fresh mushrooms	375 mL
1	medium tomato, diced	1
½ cup	finely chopped green pepper	125 mL
½ cup	finely chopped onion	125 mL
5 to 6	slices of bread, cubed	5 to 6
1½ cups	shredded cheddar cheese	375 mL
4	eggs	4
2 cups	milk	500 mL
¼ tsp	salt	1 mL
¼ tsp	freshly ground black pepper	1 mL
½ tsp	paprika	2 mL
¼ tsp	dried oregano	1 mL
¼ tsp	dried basil	1 mL

In a mixing bowl, combine mushrooms, tomato, green peppers and onions. In a greased 2-quart (2-L) casserole, layer half the bread cubes, half the vegetable mixture and half the cheese. Repeat the layers. In a mixing bowl, whisk together the eggs, milk, salt, pepper, paprika, oregano and basil. Pour over strata, cover and chill at least 3 hours or overnight.

Bake, uncovered, in a preheated 350°F (180°C) oven for 1 to 1¼ hours or until knife inserted in the center comes out clean. Serve immediately.

Makes 6 to 8 servings.

FETTUCINI AU JARDIN

A medley of fresh garden vegetables in a creamy white sauce makes this pasta dish a visually appealing, rich vegetarian entrée.

2	medium carrots	2
2	small to medium zucchini	2
1	medium yellow pepper	1
1	medium red onion, diced	1
2 tbsp	butter	25 mL
1	clove garlic, minced	1
2 tbsp	all-purpose flour	25 mL
2 cups	hot whipping cream	500 mL
½ tsp	salt	2 mL
1 tsp	freshly ground or cracked black pepper	5 mL
2 tbsp	chopped fresh basil	25 mL
1	375-g box fettucini	1
1½ cups	halved cherry tomatoes	375 mL

Julienne the carrots and zucchini. Cut the yellow pepper into 1-inch (2.5-cm) chunks. In a large saucepan, melt the butter and sauté the garlic for 1 minute. Add the flour. Stir to blend and cook for 1 minute. Whisk in the heated cream, and simmer for 3 minutes until somewhat thickened, stirring occasionally. Stir in salt, black pepper and basil.

In a vegetable steamer, steam the carrots, zucchini, pepper and onion for 2 minutes. Add to the sauce mixture and cook an additional 2 minutes. Remove from heat.

Cook pasta as directed on package. Spoon hot vegetable sauce over the pasta, and garnish with cherry tomatoes and fresh basil leaves.

Makes 6 servings.

CHAPTER SEVEN

WILD FOODS

This chapter explores recipes featuring rhubarb, fiddleheads and mushrooms, all ingredients that can be found growing wild in the woodlands and pastures of Nova Scotia.

While rhubarb is now cultivated and grown on the farms, plants from generations ago continue to proliferate near fences, behind barns and along roadways. Rhubarb is a relative of buckwheat, but there is little family resemblance. It is so tart that it is unthinkable to eat the stalk without considerable sweetening, but once the sugar, maple syrup or other sweetener is added, the resulting dish is delicious. The traditional combination of rhubarb and strawberries produces a very popular pie, and no self-respecting diner featuring homestyle cooking would omit it from the menu.

The fiddlehead, the edible uncurled frond of the ostrich fern, is the real harbinger of warm weather in the Maritimes. They poke through the just-thawed ground in the deep woods and are harvested when still curled under and tender. Cut off just below the ground, like asparagus, and trimmed of the papery outer cover, fiddleheads steam into a crunchy, flavorful dish that needs only some lemon butter to bring out the woodland taste.

Wild mushrooms come in countless varieties. They are hunted with great seriousness by bands of mycologists who guard their knowledge of woodland locations as if it were a state secret. Harvesting wild mushrooms is, for the most part, a job for the expert, since several varieties are poisonous. Those that are edible, however, such as the chanterelle, morel and boletus (the Italian porcini or French cepe) have a woodsy, uncultivated flavor that cannot be matched by any domesticated variety. Morels are the first mushroom to appear in the spring, and what luck for the fiddlehead hunter who happens upon some morels: the combination, sautéed in butter, is a truly unforgettable dish.

The orange-colored chanterelle is one wild mushroom that is often found in the farmers' markets or in gourmet groceries. Its flavor is both fruity and spicy, and it lends beautiful color when added to a dish. It does not take many to enliven a dish, so don't let the price scare you away. All wild mushrooms are only worth buying if they look good. Just because they are a wild product does not mean that they are acceptable if broken or dried out.

David Rome is a mushroom hunter–poet—a not unusual combination. In fact, when the mushroomers speak of their prey, the conversations are more passionate than one might expect when a vegetable is the topic. Charles owned a restaurant in Halifax and, one fall, invited Jasper White, the well-known chef and historian of New England cuisine, to act as guest chef at a charity benefit. Jasper loved the oysters, pheasants, pumpkins and other local ingredients supplied to him for the five-course meal. He mentioned that some wild mushrooms would be the perfect addition to one of the dishes, and David was asked for advice. After considerable quiet discussion about the menu, the flavors that would be mixed, the colors of the dish and other pertinent details, David disappeared. We have experienced this phenomenon before and assured Jasper that something was in the works. A couple of hours later, David and his very familiar hand-woven wicker basket appeared at the back door. In the basket were some almost-perfect specimens of the wild matsutake mushroom. This dense, flavorful mushroom is hugely prized in Japan and found here in the fall and early winter. Jasper was thrilled, and the diners were delighted at the combination of braised pheasant and deep matsutake-flavored sauce. David was pressed for the secret location of the mushroom patch, assumed by all to be in deep, lonely woods. After considerable pressure, he relented and told us that he had discovered them along the highway from Halifax to the airport, growing just off the side of the road. He had watched them grow over a few weeks and hoped that they would not be taken by another hunter before reaching their prime. We were the lucky ones.

RHUBARB CUSTARD PIE

The rhubarb retains a bit of crunch while surrounded by a soft, creamy custard. The sweet and sour flavor is refreshing. We offer a second variation of this recipe, using a brown-sugar-based caramel filling as an alternative.

1	pastry for a single pie crust	1
2	eggs	2
1 cup	granulated sugar	250 mL
3 tbsp	all-purpose flour	45 mL
⅛ tsp	salt	0.5 mL
½ cup	heavy or whipping cream (35%)	125 mL
3 cups	rhubarb cut into	750 mL
	½-inch (1-cm) pieces	
2 tbsp	granulated sugar	25 mL

Line a 9-inch (23-cm) pie plate with pie crust. Trim and crimp edges. Separate eggs, slightly beat yolks and set egg whites aside. In a mixing bowl, blend sugar with 2 tbsp (25 mL) flour and salt. Stir in the beaten egg yolks and cream. Stir in the rhubarb. Sprinkle the remaining 1 tbsp (15 mL) flour on the bottom of pie crust. Add the rhubarb mixture. Bake in a preheated 450°F (230°C) oven for 10 minutes, reduce the oven temperature to 350°F (180°C) for an additional 30 minutes. In a small bowl, beat the egg whites with an electric hand mixer, until soft peaks form. Gradually add the sugar and continue to beat until stiff peaks form. Spread meringue on top of pie and brown in a 350°F (180°C) oven for 5 to 10 minutes or until meringue has browned.

Makes 8 servings.

RHUBARB CARAMEL PIE

2	eggs	2
1 cup	brown sugar	250 mL
¼ cup	all-purpose flour	50 mL
2 tbsp	melted butter	25 mL
pinch	salt	pinch
2 cups	finely chopped rhubarb	500 mL
	Pastry for a single pie crust	

In a mixing bowl, lightly beat the eggs. Add the sugar, flour, butter and salt, and stir until well combined and smooth. Add the chopped rhubarb.

Line a 9-inch (23-cm) deep-dish pie plate with pastry. Add the rhubarb mixture and bake in a preheated 425°F (220°C) oven for 10 minutes. Reduce the oven temperature to 325°F (160°C) and continue to bake for an additional 30 minutes.

Makes 8 servings.

CINNAMON RHUBARB AND PEAR CRISP

Rhubarb is often combined with fruits such as strawberries. Ripe pears are an unusual match but they work well together, as the baked pear is sweet and soft and the rhubarb retains some of its tartness and a bit of its crunch.

2 cups	finely chopped rhubarb	500 mL
5	pears, peeled, cored and sliced	5
2 tbsp	all-purpose flour	25 mL
1 cup	granulated sugar	250 mL
2 tsp	ground cinnamon	10 mL
½ cup	brown sugar	125 mL
½ cup	all-purpose flour	125 mL
⅓ cup	softened butter	75 mL
¾ cup	rolled oats	175 mL

Put rhubarb and pears in a 2-quart (2-L) baking dish. Sprinkle with flour, granulated sugar and cinnamon, and gently toss to coat. In a medium-sized mixing bowl, combine brown sugar and flour. Cut in butter with a fork or pastry blender until it forms a fine crumb. Stir in the rolled oats until well combined and sprinkle over fruit mixture. Bake in a preheated 350°F (180°C) oven for 30 to 35 minutes or until bubbly. Serve warm with whipped cream.

Makes 8 servings.

RHUBARB RELISH

Relish is an unusual way of preparing rhubarb, which is most often used in desserts. The tartness of the rhubarb makes for a tangy relish that is good with pork or poultry.

4 cups	diced rhubarb	1 L
4 cups	diced onions	1 L
6 cups	brown sugar	1.5 L
2 cups	cider vinegar	500 mL
1 tsp	ground cinnamon	5 mL
½ tsp	ground cloves	2 mL
1 tsp	ground allspice	5 mL
½ tsp	pepper	2 mL
2 tsp	salt	10 mL

Measure all the ingredients into a large pot. Stir to combine. Simmer over low heat until the mixture is reduced by half and thickened, approximately 2 hours. Remove from heat and put in sterilized bottles and seal. Serve chilled.

Makes 8 cups.

RHUBARB SQUARES

The natural marriage of rhubarb and strawberries comes together in another of the many sweets that are traditionally served at tea time.

2 cups	diced rhubarb, fresh or frozen	500 mL
1 cup	strawberries, fresh or frozen	250 mL
1½ cups	granulated sugar	375 mL
½ tsp	cinnamon	2 mL
2 tbsp	cornstarch	25 mL
2 tbsp	water	25 mL
2 cups	all-purpose flour	500 mL
1½ cups	flaked coconut	375 mL
1 tsp	baking powder	5 mL
½ tsp	salt	2 mL
¾ cup	granulated sugar	175 mL
1 cup	margarine or butter	250 mL

In a saucepan over low heat, cook the rhubarb, strawberries, sugar, cinnamon, cornstarch and water until tender. Cool.

In a mixing bowl, blend flour, coconut, baking powder, salt and sugar. Cut in margarine or butter to form a fine crumb. Press one-half of the crumb mixture into the bottom of an 8 x 12 inch (20 x 30 cm) baking pan. Add rhubarb mixture and top with the remaining crumbs. Bake in a preheated 350°F (180°C) oven for 30 to 35 minutes. Chill before serving. These squares are best if kept refrigerated and they also freeze very well.

Makes 24 squares.

RHUBARB AND STRAWBERRY PINWHEELS

Rhubarb, which is found around the world, is easy to grow and will produce year after year with minimal care. This cobbler-style dessert combines tart rhubarb with sweet strawberries and is decorated with a tasty pinwheel topping.

1½ cups	granulated sugar	375 mL
7 tsp	cornstarch	35 mL
	Juice of 1 lemon	
¼ cup	water	50 mL
2 tbsp	melted butter	25 mL
2 cups	rhubarb, fresh or frozen	500 mL
1 cup	strawberries, fresh or frozen	250 mL

Pinwheels

2 cups	all-purpose flour	500 mL
4 tsp	baking powder	20 mL
1 tsp	salt	5 mL
2 tbsp	granulated sugar	25 mL
¼ cup	shortening	50 mL
1	egg	1
	Milk	
3 tbsp	softened butter	45 mL
3 tbsp	granulated sugar	45 mL
	Grated rind from 1 lemon	

In a saucepan, blend sugar and cornstarch. Add lemon juice and water and bring to a boil over high heat, stirring constantly until sugar is dissolved. Add the butter, rhubarb and strawberries, stirring to combine. Pour into a 13 x 9 inch (33 x 23 cm) pan.

Pinwheels: In a mixing bowl, blend the flour, baking powder, salt and sugar. Cut in the shortening with a pastry blender or fork to form a coarse crumb. In a 1-cup (250-mL) liquid measure, lightly beat the egg. Add enough milk to make 1 cup (250 mL). Stir into dry ingredients to make a soft dough. Turn dough out onto a lightly floured surface and roll out to ½-inch (1-cm) thick rectangle. Spread with butter. In a small bowl, stir together sugar and lemon rind. Sprinkle half over the dough. Roll jelly-roll style and cut into 8 pieces. Place pinwheels on top of the rhubarb mixture and sprinkle with remaining sugar and rind. Bake in a preheated 400°F (200°C) oven for 25 minutes. Serve warm with whipped cream or ice cream.

Makes 8 servings.

RHUBARB AND STRAWBERRY COMPOTE

Brown sugar and cinnamon bring spicy sweetness to this dessert dish. As a topping it is wonderful over regular or frozen yogurt or ice cream. For a more formal presentation, alternate layers of compote and ice cream in a parfait glass.

4 cups	diced rhubarb	1 L
¼ cup	orange juice	50 mL
1 tsp	ground cinnamon	5 mL
1 cup	brown sugar	250 mL
3 cups	sliced strawberries*	750 mL

In a saucepan, stir together the rhubarb with the orange juice, cinnamon and brown sugar. Cook until tender, approximately 6 to 8 minutes. Remove from heat and cool. Add strawberries and refrigerate.

*Fresh or frozen strawberries can be used. If using frozen berries, cut while frozen and then thaw and drain.

Makes 8 servings.

STEWED RHUBARB

A traditional breakfast dish, this simple combination of rhubarb and sugar is not too sweet. It could go alongside oatmeal or pancakes. The following recipe offers two approaches to making stewed rhubarb.

4 cups	diced rhubarb	1 L
1 cup	granulated sugar	250 mL
¼ cup	water	50 mL

In a saucepan, combine rhubarb and water. Cook, over medium heat, until the rhubarb is tender. Remove from heat. Add sugar and stir until it dissolves. The rhubarb breaks up during this cooking process and makes a soft textured sauce.

If you want the rhubarb to retain more of its shape, combine the water and sugar in a saucepan and stir to dissolve the sugar. Bring the syrup mixture to a boil. Reduce the heat and drop the pieces of rhubarb into the hot liquid. Simmer until tender. This is how Heather's Grammie Taylor cooked her rhubarb on the kitchen wood stove.

Makes 4 cups (1 L).

STEAMED FIDDLEHEADS

The curled shape, the crunch and the truly unique woodsy flavor make this simple steamed green a versatile and unusual side dish. Serve hot with butter, salt and pepper, or a lemon glaze.

2 cups	fiddleheads	500 mL

Remove the papery outer layer from the fresh fiddleheads and wash well. Put the fresh fiddleheads in a vegetable steamer over boiling water. Cover and steam 5 to 10 minutes or until tender crisp.

Lemon Butter Glaze

¼ cup	lemon juice	50 mL
¼ cup	butter	50 mL

In a small saucepan, melt the butter, and stir in the lemon juice. Pour over the steamed fiddleheads and gently toss to coat. Serve immediately.

Makes 4 servings.

FIDDLEHEAD QUICHE

Fiddleheads, the unopened fronds of the ostrich fern, are a springtime delicacy found in the woodlands of Nova Scotia. They can be purchased fresh in many supermarkets and farm markets in season or as a frozen product for year-round use.

3	eggs	3
⅔ cup	milk	150 mL
1 cup	cooked fiddleheads	250 mL
1 cup	chopped mushrooms	250 mL
1 cup	grated cheddar cheese	250 mL
2 tbsp	chopped green onions	25 mL
¼ tsp	paprika	1 mL
	Salt and pepper to taste	
	Pastry for a single pie crust	
1 tbsp	all-purpose flour	15 mL
4	slices bacon, crisply cooked and crumbled	4

In a mixing bowl, beat the eggs and stir in the milk. Add the fiddleheads, mushrooms, cheese, green onions, paprika, salt and pepper, and stir to combine. Line a 9-inch (23-cm) pie plate with pastry. Crimp and trim edges. Sprinkle pastry shell with flour. Pour in fiddlehead mixture. Top with crumbled bacon. Bake in a preheated 375°F (190°C) oven for 35 to 40 minutes or until golden brown and knife inserted in center comes out clean. Serve hot with a side salad.

Makes 8 servings.

MARINATED FIDDLEHEADS

A quick cooking of the fiddleheads keeps their bright green color and crunchy texture. This Italian-style marinade creates an antipasto dish that can be served along with a variety of cheeses, sausages and olives.

¼ cup	balsamic wine vinegar	50 mL
2 tbsp	olive oil	25 mL
½ cup	water	125 mL
1 tsp	lemon juice	5 mL
¼ tsp	salt	1 mL
1 tsp	chopped fresh parsley	5 mL
¼ tsp	dried thyme	1 mL
6	whole black peppercorns	6
1	sprig fresh rosemary	1
1	clove garlic, crushed	1
2 tbsp	chopped green onions	25 mL
1 cup	fresh fiddleheads	250 mL

In a saucepan, blend the vinegar, olive oil, water, lemon juice, salt, parsley, thyme, peppercorns and rosemary. Bring to a boil, then reduce the heat to low and simmer for 5 minutes. Add the garlic, green onions and fiddleheads. Increase the heat to high and bring to a boil. Boil for 1 minute. Remove from heat and allow to cool. Remove rosemary sprig and refrigerate in a covered glass container. May be stored for up to 2 weeks.

Makes 2 cups (500 mL).

PAN-GRILLED WILD MUSHROOMS

"Wild" is a misnomer perhaps, since shitake, portobello, enoki and other unusual mushrooms are now being cultivated. They are very different in flavor from the common white variety. Some mushrooms such as the chanterelle, matsutake and morel are still wild and can be found in season in the markets. They are extraordinary when grilled. Combine a few varieties if you can get them.

1 lb	fresh chanterelle mushrooms or other wild mushroom	500 g
½ cup	olive oil	125 mL
2	cloves garlic, finely chopped	2
	Salt and pepper to taste	
½ cup	white wine	125 mL
1 tbsp	butter	15 mL

Wipe the mushrooms clean with a damp cloth. In a large, heavy-bottomed skillet (big enough to hold all the mushrooms in one layer), heat the olive oil. Place the mushrooms top side down and brown over medium heat, about 3 minutes. Turn and continue to cook until tender throughout. Add the garlic, salt and pepper and toss, cooking for 1 additional minute. Remove the mushrooms from the pan and set aside.

Pour the wine into the hot pan. Scrape up any brown bits clinging to the bottom and bring to a boil, reducing the liquid by half. In the meantime, slice any of the mushrooms that are especially large. Whisk the butter into the wine reduction and blend well. Return mushrooms to the pan and heat through. Serve immediately.

Makes 6 servings.

CREAM OF CHANTERELLE

As far away from a can of cream of mushroom soup as you can get. If fresh chanterelles are not available when you crave this soup, buy a couple of ounces of the dried variety and reconstitute them by placing them in a small bowl and adding a cup of very hot water.

Even the cultivated white mushroom adds an earthy flavor to many dishes. They are available year round and are very affordable.

2 tsp	olive oil	10 mL
1 tbsp	chopped onion	15 mL,
½ tsp	chopped garlic	2 mL
½ lb	chanterelles, sliced	250 g
1 tsp	all-purpose flour	5 mL
2 tbsp	white wine	25 mL
3½ cups	chicken stock	875 mL
1 cup	heavy or whipping cream (35%)	250 mL
	Salt and pepper to taste	
1 tsp	chopped fresh chives	5 mL
	or parsley	

In a saucepan, heat the olive oil, then add the onion, garlic and chanterelles. Cook until the onions are transparent. Dust with the flour. Add the white wine and chicken stock. Stir to combine. Simmer for 30 minutes. Add the heavy cream and simmer for another 5 minutes. Add salt and pepper to taste. Serve in prewarmed bowls, and garnish with chopped chives or parsley.

Makes 4 servings.

We tried this soup with regular white or button mushrooms and had very satisfactory results.

MUSHROOM AND LEEK SOUP

Leeks add subtlety and depth of flavor to many dishes such as soups and stews. Alone and braised, they make a great bed for fish. Look for brightly colored green leaves and white, unblemished bulbs. After trimming the leaves, slit the stalk almost through with a vertical cut, and wash out the sand that will be hidden within.

We think that leeks are underused in the home kitchen. They are a lovely vegetable with a hint of onion and garlic. They team up nicely with the mushrooms in this smooth and delicate soup that could be a first course for a salmon entrée.

2	leeks	2
¼ cup	butter	50 mL
¼ cup	butter	50 mL
½ lb	chopped mushrooms	250 g
¼ cup	all-purpose flour	50 mL
½ tsp	salt	2 mL
	Dash of cayenne pepper	
1 cup	chicken broth	250 mL
3 cups	milk	750 mL
1 tbsp	sherry	15 mL

Wash leeks very well. Slice, using white portion only. In a saucepan, melt ¼ cup (50 mL) butter and sauté the leeks until tender. Remove leeks and reserve. Melt the second ¼ cup (50 mL) of butter in the same saucepan and sauté the mushrooms for 10 minutes or until soft. Stir in the flour, salt and cayenne pepper, coating the mushrooms. Gradually stir in the chicken stock and milk. Cook over medium heat until the mixture thickens and comes to a boil. Add the leeks and sherry. Adjust seasonings and simmer 10 minutes.

Makes 6 servings.

CHAPTER EIGHT

NATURE'S SWEETENERS

Honey and maple syrup do double duty, adding a desired sweetness to the dishes in which they are used, but, moreover, creating a dimension of flavor that can range from subtle to pronounced. The most popular, widely available honey in North America comes from bees who take nectar from clover, sage and orange blossoms. Mother Nature has made it difficult for the Nova Scotian beekeepers to take advantage of the orange blossoms, but she has supplied the more exotic nectar of blueberry blossoms and heather, which more than compensate, providing distinctly different flavors to the honey. Honey is the product of tremendous effort on the part of the honey bee. Consider that one bee, in its lifetime, flies the equivalent of a trip around the world and produces one teaspoon (5 mL) of honey. Honey is found in a variety of forms—liquid or creamed—and grades—white, golden, amber and dark. The light-colored honeys are milder in flavor; the darker honeys offer a distinctive flavor to a dish and are more often used in baking. Honey is a sensitive product that will easily pick up the flavor of other foods it is stored near. Unless you enjoy the idea of onion or garlic honey, it would be a good idea to keep the honey well sealed in the pantry. It also freezes well without losing any flavor, so, if you find a flavorful honey at a farm stand, there is no reason to worry about needing to use it up quickly. Creamed honey or honey that has become granular in the fridge can easily be liquefied by setting the container in a pan of warm water.

Maple syrup is a sweetener that was introduced to the European settlers by the Native North Americans. It is the oldest agricultural crop in the Maritimes, and the techniques of converting the sap to syrup and sugar were developed by the aboriginal residents of Eastern Canada. They used hollowed-out logs, which were filled with the contents of the sap buckets. Large stones were heated in a firepit until very hot, and then thrown into the log, sending up great plumes of sweet-scented steam that filled the woods. Not as efficient as today's methods, but it must have been a great event.

Sugar maples are tapped for their sap during a very short, three- to six-week season in the spring. The daytime temperatures need to be above 40°F (4°C) and the nights in the low 20s (above -6°C). When that happens in March, the maple camps get into full swing, and the cry "Sap's running" can be heard around the province. Sap can be collected by hanging buckets on the tapped trees or by the newer method of running plastic tubing from the tree to the sugar house. Either way, the end product is a thick, rich syrup that, once you've tasted it, will forever put you off the maple-flavored corn syrup that masquerades as the real thing.

We spent much of a day with George and Phyllis Cook, whose Mapleridge Farm is the largest, independently owned sugarbush in Nova Scotia. (There are currently 70 producers around the province.) The farm is nestled on the Cobequid Mountains, three miles (5 km) off the main road of the village of Central New Annan (and, yes, we have an East and a West New Annan as well). The Cobequids are covered with meadows and forests, and offer beautiful views of the Northumberland Strait, which separates Nova Scotia from Prince Edward Island. Mapleridge is a big operation, with more than 23,000 trees tapped using the newest method of gravity-feeding the sap through plastic tubes to the oil-fired evaporator. The tubes make the collection of sap much easier but offer a huge temptation to the squirrels and bears that inhabit the mountains. Since they share the human sweet tooth, and gnaw holes in the plastic tubing, vigilance on the part of the farmer is essential. George, Phyllis and about a dozen employees can manage the sugarbush, where it takes 40 gallons (160 L) of sap to make a gallon (4 L) of syrup. We learned that trees produce sap until they reach about 250 years of age. Most of the Cooks' trees were planted just before the turn of the century, so their sugarbush has barely reached middle age. In order to protect the health of the maples, the tap needs to be moved around the tree from season to season to maximize the sap collection. Larger trees (15–19 inches/38–48 cm around) can handle two taps. It takes about five years for the tap hole to heal. We were amused to learn that Phyllis, who is English, was not fond of maple syrup when she arrived in Canada, but that soon changed. Now, she and George can't recall a morning when breakfast has not included maple syrup on oatmeal porridge. We prevailed upon Phyllis to share with us the wonderful Maple Pecan Squares recipe that appears in this book.

Maple syrup forms the basis for other products such as granulated maple sugar, maple butter and maple candy. The sugar season marks the beginning of many months of food festivals in Nova Scotia, celebrating a wide variety of products from the farm and the sea. Maple suppers, with sausages, pancakes and desserts all featuring the fresh syrup, are found in community halls, churches and fire stations from mid-March to mid-April. They are often billed as fund-raisers. However, considering the huge plates of food that are sold for a few dollars, it seems to us that the suppers are more a way for the neighbors to emerge from a long winter's hibernation and share a good time and good food with friends.

HONEYED APPLES AND CRANBERRIES

The sweet and tart combination of ingredients in this condiment accompanies roasted pork, poultry or lamb very well. It is equally tasty whether the meat is hot or cold, and the brightly colored apple wedges make for an appealing plate.

In past civilizations, honey has been offered to the gods and used to pay taxes.

4	medium apples	4
2 cups	cranberries	500 mL
1 cup	water	250 mL
½ cup	liquid honey	125 mL
¾ cup	granulated sugar	175 mL
¼ tsp	salt	1 mL
2	cinnamon sticks (optional)	2

Peel and core apples. Either cut into wedges or in half. In a saucepan, bring to a gentle boil the apples, cranberries and water. Reduce heat, cover and simmer for 5 minutes. Gently turn apples to obtain an even red color. Add remaining ingredients and continue to cook over low heat until apples are tender, 15 to 20 minutes. Chill before serving.

To serve, carefully remove apples and arrange on serving dishes. Top with cranberry mixture.

Makes 4 servings.

HONEY CRANBERRY RELISH

This interesting variation on traditional cranberry sauce makes a delicious accompaniment to poultry or pork entrées. Try it on toast for an eye-opening taste at breakfast time.

2 cups	cranberries	500 mL
½ cup	liquid honey	125 mL
1	orange, peeled and diced	1
2	whole cloves (optional)	2

In a saucepan, combine all ingredients. Cook over high heat, stirring frequently for 7 to 9 minutes, or until cranberries pop open. Cool. Store refrigerated in a covered container. Serve with meat or poultry.

Makes 2 cups (500 mL).

Honey Tips:

Honey will slide out of measuring spoons and cups easily if they are rinsed in hot water first.

Light-colored, mild-flavored honey is best used to enhance the flavors of other foods, while darker, stronger-flavored honey gives a distinctive sweetness to baked goods.

Baked goods made with honey tend to stay moist due to honey's hygroscopic or moisture-absorbing ability.

All liquid honey will eventually granulate or go hard, but it can be returned to a liquid state by placing the container in warm water.

HONEY OATMEAL RAISIN BREAD

We have added honey and rolled oats to this traditional "raisin bread," a favorite after-school snack. This bread is wonderful when toasted and buttered.

4 cups	boiling water	1 L
2 cups	rolled oats	500 mL
½ cup	liquid honey	125 mL
1 cup	raisins	250 mL
¼ cup	vegetable oil	50 mL
¼ cup	liquid honey	50 mL
1 cup	warm water	250 mL
3 tbsp	dry yeast	45 mL
1 cup	all-purpose flour	250 mL
3 tbsp	salt	45 mL
7 to 8 cups	all-purpose flour	1.75 to 2 L

In a large bowl, add the boiling water to the rolled oats, honey, raisins and oil. Stir until well combined and allow to cool to lukewarm. In a small bowl, add the honey to the warm water, stirring until the honey is dissolved. Add yeast, and stir to mix. Cover and set aside for 5 minutes. Then add 1 cup (250 mL) flour. Stir until smooth. Let stand for 10 minutes or until bubbly. Add the yeast mixture to the oatmeal, stirring to combine. Add the salt and the flour 1 cup (250 mL) at a time until dough comes away clean from the sides of the bowl. Turn dough out onto a floured surface and knead until smooth and elastic. Place in a greased bowl, cover and let rise for 70 minutes or until double in bulk. Punch down and let rise again for 60 minutes or until double in bulk. Punch down and divide dough into four equal pieces. Shape into loaves and place in greased 9 x 5 inch (23 x 12 cm) loaf pans. Cover and let rise until dough is slightly above the edge of the pan. Bake in a preheated 325°F (160°C) oven for 40 to 50 minutes.

Makes 4 loaves.

MAPLE PECAN SQUARES

Maple sap collected straight from the trees was often used as a spring tonic in earlier times.

Pecans have a toasty and rich taste that loves to be paired with an equally rich sweetener such as brown sugar or, as in this recipe, maple syrup. If you happen to have any left, cover with plastic wrap and refrigerate.

Base

1 cup	all-purpose flour	250 mL
¼ cup	brown sugar	50 mL
½ cup	butter, softened	125 mL

Topping

1 cup	pure maple syrup	250 mL
⅔ cup	brown sugar	150 mL
2	eggs, beaten	2
¼ cup	butter, softened	50 mL
¼ tsp	salt	1 mL
½ tsp	vanilla	2 mL
2 tbsp	all-purpose flour	25 mL
⅔ cup	pecan halves	150 mL

Base: In a small bowl, combine flour and sugar. Rub in butter to form a fine crumb. Press mixture evenly into the bottom of a 7 x 11 inch (16 x 27 cm) greased pan. Bake in a preheated 350°F (180°C) oven for 5 minutes.

Topping: In a saucepan, combine maple syrup and sugar. Simmer over medium heat for 5 minutes, stirring to dissolve the sugar into the maple syrup. Cool slightly. In a mixing bowl, whisk the maple mixture into the beaten eggs. Stir in remaining ingredients, except the pecans. Spread evenly over base, then top with pecan halves. Bake in a preheated 450°F (230°C) oven for 10 minutes. Reduce oven temperature to 350°F (180°C) and bake an additional 20 minutes. Cool and cut into squares.

Makes 32 squares.

MAPLE SYRUP CAKE

A simple, very old recipe that relies on maple syrup as the primary flavoring. It is a moist cake that doesn't really need an icing but the maple cream cheese icing used on the carrot squares from page 93 complements this cake.

Lighter colored syrup is the mildest in flavor and the highest grade, while darker colored syrups have a stronger flavor and are recommended for baking and cooking.

½ cup	shortening	125 mL
½ cup	granulated sugar	125 mL
1 tsp	vanilla extract	5 mL
½ cup	pure maple syrup	125 mL
2	eggs, lightly beaten	2
1¾ cups	all-purpose flour	425 mL
2½ tsp	baking powder	12 mL
½ tsp	salt	2 mL
¼ cup	milk	50 mL
½ cup	chopped nuts	125 mL

In a mixing bowl, cream shortening, sugar and vanilla until well blended. Gradually beat in maple syrup. Add beaten eggs to mixture. Stir until well blended. In a small mixing bowl, combine flour, baking powder and salt. Alternately add the dry ingredients and the milk to the maple mixture until well blended and smooth. Fold in nuts.

Pour batter into a greased 8 x 8 inch (20 x 20 cm) baking pan and bake in a preheated 350°F (180°C) oven for 45 minutes or until tester inserted in the cake comes out clean. Cool.

Makes 16 pieces.

MAPLE NUT MUFFINS

We have teamed up the taste of maple syrup and ground cardamom to provide the exceptional flavor of these muffins.

¼ cup	melted butter	50 mL
⅓ cup	pure maple syrup	75 mL
⅔ cup	milk	150 mL
1	egg, lightly beaten	1
½ tsp	maple or vanilla extract	2 mL
1 cup	all-purpose flour	250 mL
¾ cup	whole-wheat flour	175 mL
1 tbsp	baking powder	15 mL
½ tsp	salt	2 mL
¼ tsp	ground cinnamon	1 mL
¼ tsp	ground cardamom	1 mL
½ cup	chopped walnuts	125 mL

Crumb Topping

1 tbsp	granulated sugar	15 mL
1 tbsp	brown sugar	15 mL
¼ cup	finely chopped walnuts	50 mL
¼ tsp	cinnamon	1 mL

In a small bowl, combine melted butter, maple syrup, milk, egg and maple or vanilla extract. In another mixing bowl, combine the all-purpose and whole-wheat flours, baking powder, salt, cinnamon and cardamom. Add liquid mixture to dry ingredients taking care not to over-mix. Fold in nuts. Fill greased muffin tins two-thirds full with batter.

Crumb Topping: In a small bowl combine all the topping ingredients and stir to blend. Sprinkle over each muffin. Bake in a preheated 425°F (220°C) oven for 15 to 20 minutes.

Makes 12 muffins.

MAPLE SYRUP PIE

Pure maple syrup and cream—this heavenly
combination stands alone in a flaky pie crust to make a
memorable dessert that could not be simpler to prepare.

1½ cups	pure maple syrup	375 mL
1 cup	heavy or whipping cream (35%)	250 mL
⅓ cup	cornstarch	75 mL
¼ cup	cold water	50 mL
1	9-inch (23-cm) baked single pie crust	1

In a saucepan, combine maple syrup and cream. In a small bowl, dissolve the cornstarch in the water. Add to maple mixture, and stir until well blended. Over medium heat, bring the maple mixture to a boil, and cook for 2 minutes, stirring constantly until thickened.

Remove from heat and pour into baked pie crust. Cool until set.

Makes 8 to 10 servings.

MAPLE SPREAD

| ½ cup | softened cream cheese | 125 g |
| ¼ cup | maple syrup | 50 mL |

In a mixing bowl, beat the cream cheese until light and smooth. Add the maple syrup and continue to beat until well combined.

Spread on toast or crackers.

Makes 1/2 cup (125 mL)

MAPLE FRENCH TOAST

Storing tips for maple syrup: Maple syrup can be stored in the freezer for up to one year, where it will become very thick but not lose any flavor. Tightly sealed, unopened containers can be stored in a cool dry place for 6 months. Once opened, containers should be closed tightly and stored in the refrigerator.

When it comes to pure maple syrup, there's no such thing as too much. Adding syrup to the batter makes for unforgettable French toast.

3	eggs	3
½ cup	pure maple syrup	125 mL
1 cup	milk	250 mL
¼ cup	light cream (18%)	50 mL
dash	ground nutmeg	dash
	Pinch of salt	
6 to 8	slices of bread	6 to 8

In a mixing bowl, whisk together the eggs and the maple syrup. Add the milk, cream, nutmeg and salt. Whisk until well combined. Dip the bread, one slice at a time, into the maple mixture, turning once to coat both sides. Drain and fry in a hot buttered pan on both sides until browned.

Serve hot, topped with warmed maple syrup.

Makes 3 to 4 servings.

MAPLE SPICED SQUASH

Yellow and orange root vegetables such as squash and carrots pair beautifully with the rich flavor of maple. Winter squash, such as acorn and butternut, are no exception. Try this squash side dish alongside roasted meats.

2	medium butternut or acorn squash	2
¼ cup	butter	50 mL
¼ cup	finely chopped onion	50 mL
¼ tsp	ground nutmeg	1 mL
¼ tsp	salt	1 mL
⅛ tsp	white pepper	0.5 mL
½ cup	water	125 mL
⅓ cup	pure maple syrup	75 mL

Cut the squash in half and remove seeds. Place each half, cut side up, on a baking sheet and bake in a preheated 400°F (200°C) oven for 1 hour or until tender. Allow to cool slightly. Using a large spoon, scoop out the squash flesh and set aside.

In a heavy-bottomed saucepan, melt the butter over medium heat. Add the onions, nutmeg, salt and pepper and sauté until onions are soft. Add to the reserved squash, and stir to combine. Add water and maple syrup. In a food processor, purée until mixture is smooth. Adjust salt and pepper to taste. Return to saucepan and reheat over low heat.

Makes 4 to 6 servings.

MAPLE GLAZED CARROTS

Our native Mi'mqak converted maple syrup to sugar as it was easier to store and barter with for other goods.

Maple and butter together make this shiny glaze that coats the carrot slices and brings out the natural sweetness of this common root vegetable.

3 cups	sliced carrots	750 mL
2 tbsp	pure maple syrup	25 mL
1 tbsp	melted butter	15 mL
	Salt and pepper to taste	

In a saucepan, cook the carrots until they are tender crisp, approximately 10 minutes. In a small bowl, blend the maple syrup and butter. Drain the cooked carrots. Add the maple syrup mixture and stir to coat. Season with salt and pepper to taste.

Makes 4 to 6 servings.

MAPLE SYRUP ON THE SNOW

This maple treat is a favorite during the sugaring-off parties held at maple camps throughout the province.

Heat the pure maple syrup to 236°F (113°C) for soft taffy or to 250°F (120°C) for hard taffy. The hot syrup is then poured into strips onto well-packed clean snow and eaten with a fork or stick. Crushed ice may be used instead of snow for a year-round treat.

MAPLE-BERRY SHAKE

The color is purple and the maple and blueberry flavors sparkle.
Use low-fat ice cream and milk as an alternative. In either case,
this shake is an exceptionally refreshing summer drink.

1 cup	cold milk	250 mL
¼ cup	pure maple syrup	50 mL
½ cup	blueberries, fresh or frozen	125 mL
1 cup	vanilla ice cream	250 mL

Place all ingredients in a blender and blend until smooth. Pour into chilled glasses and enjoy.

Makes 2 servings.

HONEY SAUCE

A perfect topper for fresh fruit.

¼ cup	liquid honey	50 mL
1 cup	sour cream	250 mL

In a small bowl, whisk together the honey and sour cream until smooth. Drizzle over fresh fruit for a real taste sensation.

Makes 1¼ cups (300 mL).

MAPLE BASTED CHICKEN

Sweet maple and tangy mustard and vinegar combine to make this non-traditional barbecue sauce. The sugar in the syrup will produce a golden brown coating, but be sure to turn the chicken frequently to keep the sauce from burning.

⅓ cup	pure maple syrup	75 mL
1	medium onion, finely diced	1
2	cloves garlic, finely diced	2
2 tbsp	cider vinegar	25 mL
1 tbsp	Dijon mustard	15 mL
2 tbsp	vegetable oil	25 mL
	Salt and pepper to taste	
4	6-oz (180-g) boneless, skinless chicken breasts	4

In a mixing bowl, whisk the maple syrup, onion, garlic, cider vinegar, mustard, oil and salt and pepper until well blended. Add the chicken pieces and toss to coat. Cover and refrigerate for 1 to 2 hours.

Heat the grill until the coals are hot. Oil the rack. Remove chicken from the marinade and reserve excess marinade for basting. Place chicken on rack and grill until it has lost it pinkness. Turn every few minutes and brush with reserved marinade.

Makes 4 servings.

This dish may also be prepared in the oven. Place chicken in a covered casserole dish and cook in a preheated 375°F (190°C) oven for 35 to 40 minutes.

BOULARDERIE'S BISCUITS

*Boularderie Island on Bras D'Or Lake, Cape Breton, is
the location of some old Nova Scotia farms and a
popular spot for summer cottages. These biscuits are
biscuit size and shape but taste more like a molasses
cookie. Once you have eaten one, you will know why they
are made thick like a biscuit—a smaller cookie just
would not be enough.*

½ cup	shortening	125 mL
1 cup	molasses	250 mL
1 tsp	baking soda	5 mL
1	egg, slightly beaten	1
2½ cups	all-purpose flour	625 mL
1 tsp	ground cinnamon	5 mL
1 tsp	ground ginger	5 mL
½ tsp	allspice	2 mL
½ tsp	ground cloves	2 mL
	Pinch of salt	
½ cup	raisins (optional)	125 mL

In a saucepan, melt shortening and add molasses. Bring to a boil,
and remove from heat. Stir in the baking soda, which will cause the
mixture to foam up; set aside to cool. Once cooled, beat in egg. In a
small bowl, blend the flour, cinnamon, ginger, allspice, cloves, salt
and raisins. Stir dry ingredients into the molasses mixture to form a
soft dough. Turn dough out onto a lightly floured surface and either
roll out or pat out with your hands until it is ½ inch (1 cm) thick.
Cut with a 2½-inch (6-cm) biscuit cutter or the floured rim of a
glass. Place biscuits 1 inch (2.5 cm) apart on an ungreased baking
sheet. Bake in a preheated 375°F (190°C) oven for 10 to 12
minutes.

Makes 18 biscuits.

BUTTERSCOTCH PIE

Our traditional butterscotch pie recipe is at least four generations old and in recent years has been adapted for the microwave. It is truly an example of how simple ingredients, in the right proportions, create the most delicious results.

Filling

4	egg yolks, lightly beaten	4
2 cups	brown sugar	500 mL
8 tbsp	all-purpose flour	120 mL
	Pinch of salt	
2 tbsp	butter	25 mL
1 tsp	vanilla extract	5 mL
3 cups	milk	750 mL

Meringue

4	egg whites	4
2 tsp	granulated sugar	10 mL
¼ tsp	vanilla extract	1 mL
	Prebaked deep-dish pie shell	

Filling: Separate eggs, lightly beat yolks and set aside the whites. In a double boiler, whisk together all the filling ingredients until smooth. Cook over medium heat until thickened. To prepare in the microwave, place the filling mixture in a microwave-safe bowl and cook on high for 12 to 15 minutes until thickened, stirring every 3 minutes during the cooking process. Remove from heat and pour into a prebaked 9-inch (23-cm) deep-dish pie shell.

Meringue: In a small bowl, beat the 4 egg whites with an electric hand mixer until soft peaks form. Gradually add the sugar and vanilla and continue to beat until stiff peaks form. Spoon on top of butterscotch filling. Bake in a preheated 350°F (180°C) oven for 5 to 10 minutes or until the meringue has browned.

Makes 8 servings.

CHAPTER NINE

BLUEBERRIES

Blueberries love acidic, sandy soil, and thrive in a mostly temperate climate that may experience big temperature swings from summer to winter. This makes Nova Scotia a perfect host for these blue-black, sweet berries. In fact, the wild blueberry is our most lucrative agricultural export crop. Blueberries cover more acreage of our province than any other farm product. Oxford, Nova Scotia, is considered to be the blueberry capital of the world, and if it has any competition, we don't know about it. Oxford is the center of blueberry festivals, jumping-off point to the "U-pick" farms, and home to the processers and exporters. For centuries, wild low-bush blueberry plants, barely a foot (30 cm) high, were all that one saw in the fields. These hardy, thick-stemmed plants producing a sweet berry are found throughout Atlantic Canada, Quebec and Maine. They grow in vast fields that are carpeted in pink and white blossoms in the spring, moving to a sea of blue in the summer, and fiery red after the first frost in the fall. Now some farmers are also growing the high-bush variety, on bushes that are more like trees, growing to 15 feet (4.5 m). The high-bush berries are easier to pick since they are well off the ground. The low-bush "wild" berries are mostly harvested by hand, using the "stoop and scoop" method. The picker carries a rake and bucket to the field, although mechanical pickers are becoming more widely used.

Look for plump, fresh-looking blueberries. The powdery cast, or bloom, is not a problem, and actually is a naturally occurring waxy coating that inhibits spoilage. Like other berries, they stop ripening as soon as they are picked. The blueberries should not be washed until ready to use. Kept dry, they should last in the refrigerator for two or three days. (Be sure to look for any soft berries and remove them before storing as they will spoil the rest.) Blueberries work really well with modern quick-freezing techniques, and the frozen berry is available year round. Individually quick-frozen blueberries keep up to two years and still maintain their taste and texture. In fact, only about three percent of the Nova Scotia harvest is eaten fresh; all the rest is frozen first.

As they did with many of the local wild fruits and vegetables, the Mi'kmaq, the original Nova Scotians, used blueberries in a very creative way. They picked the ripe, wild berries, formed them into small "pocket cakes" and dried them in the sun. The result was a portable meal that retained the high vitamin C content that the berry is known for. The cakes provided handy nourishment on fishing and hunting trips. The Mi'kmaq also added dried berries to soups and stews in the winter. We have expanded on the Mi'kmaq repertoire, but have based many of the recipes on their idea of using the berry as both a sweet snack and an ingredient in savory dishes. The berries combine well with a variety of spices, especially cardamom, cinnamon, coriander, ginger, mace and nutmeg. However, despite all our creativity, it is hard to imagine improving upon a dish of fresh, ripe blueberries with a splash of cream. That might just be the perfect dessert.

BLUEBERRY LEMON LOAF

*The tartness of lemon combined with the sweet taste of
blueberries make this loaf so popular it will
disappear very quickly.*

½ cup	softened butter	125 mL
1 cup	granulated sugar	250 mL
2	eggs	2
1¼ cups	all purpose flour	375 mL
¼ tsp	salt	1 mL
1 tsp	baking powder	5 mL
	Grated rind of 1 lemon	
½ cup	milk	125 mL
½ cup	wild blueberries, fresh or frozen	125 mL

In a bowl, cream butter and stir in sugar a little at a time. Beat in
eggs. In a small bowl, combine flour, salt, baking powder and lemon
rind. Add flour mixture alternately with milk to the butter mixture;
blend until smooth. Fold in blueberries; if using frozen blueberries,
dust lightly with all-purpose flour. Place in a greased 10 x 6 inch
(25 x 15 cm) loaf pan. Bake in a preheated 350°F (180°C) oven for
1 hour.

Topping

| ¼ cup | granulated sugar | 50 mL |
| | Juice of 1 lemon | |

In a small bowl, mix sugar and lemon juice until sugar is dissolved.
Remove baked loaf from pan and spoon topping over the hot loaf.

Makes 1 loaf.

BLUEBERRY BRAN MUFFINS

Use low-fat yogurt and milk to reduce the fat content in this and other recipes.

Blueberry bran muffins are a great way to start your day or to munch as a snack on the run. These hearty muffins combine bran, oats and whole-wheat flour with the tang of regular or low-fat plain yogurt and the sweetness of the wild blueberry.

1	egg	1
2 cups	plain yogurt	500 mL
½ cup	milk	125 mL
½ cup	molasses	125 mL
3 tbsp	brown sugar	45 mL
¼ cup	melted butter	50 mL
1 cup	all-purpose flour	250 mL
1 cup	whole-wheat flour	250 mL
1¼ cups	bran	300 mL
½ cup	rolled oats	125 mL
1¼ tsp	baking soda	6 mL
¼ tsp	salt	1 mL
½ tsp	ground cinnamon	2 mL
¼ tsp	ground nutmeg	1 mL
¼ tsp	ground ginger	1 mL
1½ cups	wild blueberries	375 mL

In a mixing bowl, beat the egg. Add the yogurt, milk, molasses, sugar and butter. Mix until well blended. In a small bowl, blend the all-purpose and whole-wheat flour, bran, oats, baking soda, salt, cinnamon, nutmeg and ginger. Add the dry ingredients to the yogurt mixture, stirring just enough to wet dry ingredients, and being very careful not to over-mix. Carefully fold in blueberries. Fill greased muffin tins three-quarters full. Bake in a preheated 425°F (220°C) oven for 15 to 20 minutes.

Makes 18 muffins.

BLUEBERRY COTTAGE PUDDING

This recipe has been passed down from generation to generation, which serves as a credit to its good taste, especially when served with the sweet brown sauce.

It has been said that the wonderful thing about tradition is that it helps us hold onto the past and create the future.

¼ cup	shortening	50 mL
½ cup	granulated sugar	125 mL
1	egg	1
½ tsp	vanilla extract	2 mL
1 cup	all-purpose flour	250 mL
2 tsp	baking powder	10 mL
¼ tsp	salt	1 mL
½ cup	milk	125 mL
1 cup	blueberries, fresh or frozen	250 mL

Cream together the shortening and sugar until light and fluffy. Add egg and vanilla, and mix well. In a small bowl, blend the flour, baking powder and salt. Add dry ingredients alternately with the milk to the sugar mixture until well blended. Dust blueberries with a small amount of flour and stir into batter. Bake in a greased 9-inch (23-cm) square baking pan in a preheated 350°F (180°C) oven for 25 to 30 minutes. Serve hot with a sweet brown sauce.

Sweet Brown Sauce

2 tbsp	butter	25 mL
2 tbsp	all-purpose flour	25 mL
¼ tsp	salt	1 mL
⅓ cup	brown sugar	75 mL
1 cup	boiling water	250 mL
¼ tsp	vanilla extract	1 mL

In a small saucepan, melt butter; add the flour and salt and stir until smooth. Add sugar, stirring constantly until browned. Remove from heat. Add boiling water, stirring until smooth. Return to medium high heat and bring back to a boil. Remove from heat and stir in the vanilla. Serve hot.

Makes 9 servings.

BLUEBERRY MAPLE SCONES

*Scones, a true
Scottish treat, are
perfectly paired
with butter and jam
or honey. The word
can be pronounced
with a long o as in
"cone" or a short o
as in "on." It comes
from the Gaelic and
refers to the "Stone
of Destiny," where
the Scottish
coronations took
place. It is the
shape, rather than
the texture, that
ought to be stone-
like.*

*Scones are the famous Scottish sweet biscuit known as
the best treat to have with strong tea on a chilly
afternoon. The blueberry and maple are certainly a local
addition to the ancestral recipe. For an unforgettable
treat, we recommend serving the Blueberry Maple Apple
Butter, on the next page, with the scones.*

¼ cup	granulated sugar	50 mL
3 cups	all-purpose flour	750 mL
1 tsp	baking powder	5 mL
½ tsp	salt	2 mL
½ cup	butter	125 mL
1	egg, beaten	1
¼ cup	pure maple syrup	50 mL
¾ cup	buttermilk*	175 mL
1 cup	blueberries, fresh or frozen	250 mL

In a mixing bowl, combine sugar, flour, baking powder and salt. Cut
in the butter with a pastry blender or fork until the mixture
resembles coarse crumbs. In separate bowl, mix together the egg,
maple syrup and buttermilk. Add the blueberries to the dry
ingredients; if using frozen blueberries, use directly from the freezer
and dust with flour. Using a fork, combine the liquid with the dry
ingredients. Turn dough out onto a lightly floured surface and gently
knead 10 to 12 times. Roll out the dough or pat out with your hand
to form a square, ½ inch (1 cm) in thickness. Cut into squares the
size of your choice. Cut each square to make 2 triangles. Place them
on an ungreased baking sheet and bake in a preheated 400°F
(200°C) oven for 10 to 12 minutes or until lightly browned.

*The buttermilk may be replaced with half and half (10%) cream.

Makes 24 large or 36 small scones.

BLUEBERRY MAPLE APPLE BUTTER

Apple butter is another of the traditional treats returning to the pantry. The addition of blueberries and maple updates this old-time favorite. The buttery spread is terrific on scones or toasted oatmeal bread.

4	large cooking apples	4
½ cup	water	125 mL
4 cups	wild blueberries	1 L
½ cup	water	125 mL
¼ cup	granulated sugar	50 mL
¼ cup	pure maple syrup	50 mL
½ tsp	salt	2 mL
1 tsp	allspice	5 mL
½ tsp	ground ginger	2 mL
dash	ground cloves	dash

Core and wedge apples. Cook with ½ cup (125 mL) water until apples are soft. Pass apples through a sieve to remove the skins. Using a blender or food processor, purée the blueberries with ½ cup (125 mL) of water. In a saucepan, combine the blueberry and apple mixtures. Stir in the sugar, maple syrup, salt, allspice, ginger and cloves. Bring to a boil. Reduce heat and simmer until smooth and thick (about 20 minutes). Pour into hot sterilized jars and seal.

Makes 4 cups (1 L).

BLUEBERRY GINGERBREAD

For blueberry ginger cupcakes: Spoon the batter into lined or greased muffin tins. Bake in a preheated 350°F (180°C) oven for approximately 20 minutes or until done. Makes 12 cupcakes.

Ginger, nutmeg and molasses are tropical ingredients that came to northern kitchens in the 1700s as a result of the active trade routes with the Caribbean Islands. The blueberries add flavor and moistness to this traditional gingerbread recipe.

½ cup	butter or margarine	125 mL
½ cup	brown sugar	125 mL
2	eggs, beaten	2
2 cups	all-purpose flour	500 mL
1 tbsp	baking powder	15 mL
¼ tsp	salt	1 mL
2 tsp	ground ginger	10 mL
1 tsp	ground cinnamon	5 mL
½ cup	sour cream	125 mL
½ cup	molasses	125 mL
1½ cups	wild blueberries, fresh or frozen	375 mL

In a mixing bowl, cream butter or margarine. Gradually add the sugar and eggs, mixing well. In a separate bowl, blend the flour, baking powder, salt, ginger and cinnamon. In a small mixing bowl, stir together the sour cream and molasses until smooth. Alternately add the flour and molasses mixtures to the creamed mixture. Dust the blueberries with flour and fold into the batter.

Pour the batter into a greased and floured 8-inch (20-cm) square baking pan. Bake in a preheated 350°F (180°C) oven for 45 minutes.

Makes 6 to 8 servings.

WILD BLUEBERRY FLAN

This cross between a cake and a pie is served chilled and can be made ahead. The orange flavor enhances the sweetness of the blueberries and the tang of the sour cream. Because this is a rich dessert, small portions will satisfy.

When baking with frozen blueberries, use them directly from the freezer unless otherwise specified in the recipe.

Crust

1½ cups	all-purpose flour	375 mL
½ cup	granulated sugar	125 mL
1 tsp	baking powder	5 mL
½ cup	softened butter or margarine	125 mL
1	egg	1
½ tsp	almond extract	2 mL

Filling

5 cups	wild blueberries, fresh or frozen	1.25 L
2 tbsp	orange juice or liqueur	25 mL
2 tbsp	minute tapioca	25 mL
1 tsp	grated lemon rind	5 mL
2 cups	sour cream	500 mL
2	egg yolks	2
½ cup	granulated sugar	125 mL
½ tsp	almond extract	2 mL

Crust: In a small mixing bowl, blend flour, sugar and baking powder. Cut in the butter; stir in the egg and almond extract to make a soft dough. Press dough into the bottom and halfway up the sides of a 9-inch (23-cm) springform pan.

Filling: In a small bowl, mix together blueberries, orange juice or liqueur, tapioca and lemon rind. Spoon into crust. In a small bowl, whisk together the sour cream, egg yolks, sugar and almond extract, stirring until well blended and smooth. Spoon over the blueberry mixture. Bake in a preheated 350°F (180°C) oven for 1 to 1¼ hours or until set. Remove from oven and cool on a wire rack.

Serve chilled, topped with whipped cream.

Makes 15 servings.

POLKA DOT CREAM

This is a simple but elegant dessert that can be eaten on its own or used as a topping.

1 cup	whipping cream	250 mL
	Granulated sugar to taste	
	Fresh blueberries	

In a mixing bowl, whip the cream with a hand electric mixer. Add sugar to taste. Fold in as many fresh blueberries as the whipped cream will hold. Chill until ready to serve—and enjoy.

WILD BLUEBERRY FUNGY

Fungy is one of those culinary words of unknown origin. It refers to a fruit dessert cooked under spoonfuls of a sweetened dumpling. Readers of our first book will recall the blueberry grunt recipe, which is somewhat similar to the fungy.

4 cups	wild blueberries, fresh or frozen	1 L
1 cup	granulated sugar	250 mL
¼ tsp	ground cinnamon	1 mL
¼ tsp	ground nutmeg	1 mL
2 cups	all-purpose flour	500 mL
¼ cup	granulated sugar	50 mL
2 tsp	baking powder	10 mL
1 tsp	salt	5 mL
½ cup	shortening	125 mL
¾ cup	milk	175 mL
¼ cup	water	50 mL

In an 8-cup (2-L) baking dish, toss blueberries with sugar, cinnamon and nutmeg. In a mixing bowl, blend the flour, sugar, baking powder and salt. Cut in shortening and add the milk to make a soft biscuit-like dough. Pour the water over the blueberry mixture and top with spoonfuls of the dough mixture. Dust the top with cinnamon sugar if you like. Bake in a preheated 350°F (180°C) oven for 25 minutes or until topping is golden brown. Serve hot.

Makes 6 to 8 servings.

BLUEBERRY BUCKLE

Native peoples used dried blueberries for medicinal purposes (for coughs, morning sickness and as a headache remedy) and to preserve venison.

Buckles are traditional desserts popular in the Maritimes and New England. The three layers of cake, fruit and crumb topping are appealing, especially when served with whipped cream, ice cream or frozen yogurt.

¼ cup	shortening	50 mL
½ cup	granulated sugar	125 mL
1	egg	1
1 cup	all-purpose flour	250 mL
1½ tsp	baking powder	7 mL
¼ tsp	salt	1 mL
⅓ cup	milk	75 mL
2 cups	blueberries, fresh or frozen	500 mL

Crumb Topping

½ cup	granulated sugar	125 mL
⅓ cup	all-purpose flour	75 mL
½ tsp	ground cinnamon	2 mL
¼ cup	butter	50 mL

In a mixing bowl, using an electric hand mixer, cream together the shortening, sugar and egg. Beat in flour, baking powder, salt and milk until mixture is well blended and smooth. Spread dough into a greased 9-inch (23-cm) square baking pan. Spread blueberries evenly over dough.

Crumb Topping: In a small mixing bowl, blend sugar, flour and cinnamon. Cut in butter with a fork or pastry blender until it resembles small crumbs. Spread crumbs evenly over blueberries.

Bake in a preheated 350°F (180°C) oven for 35 minutes. Serve warm with whipped cream or ice cream.

Makes 6 to 8 servings.

BLUEBERRY SQUARES

These squares are easy to make and are like bite-sized cheesecakes. Make them ahead and freeze for use at an upcoming party. Thaw them in the refrigerator for several hours and, before serving, top them with whipped cream.

Base

1½ cups	graham wafer crumbs	375 mL
¼ cup	granulated sugar	50 mL
½ cup	butter or margarine	125 mL

Filling

8 oz	cream cheese, softened	250 g
2	eggs	2
1 tsp	vanilla extract	5 mL
½ cup	granulated sugar	125 mL

Topping

2 tbsp	cornstarch	25 mL
½ cup	granulated sugar	125 mL
2 tbsp	water	25 mL
2 tbsp	lemon juice	25 mL
3 cups	blueberries, fresh or frozen	750 mL

Base: In a small bowl, combine graham wafer crumbs and sugar. Cut in butter to make a fine crumb. Press into the bottom of a 9 x 13 inch (23 x 33 cm) baking pan.

Filling: In a small bowl, using a hand-held electric mixer, beat the cream cheese until smooth and fluffy. Beat in the eggs, followed by the vanilla and sugar. Spread the cream cheese mixture evenly over the crumb base. Bake in a preheated 300°F (150°C) oven for 30 minutes. Cool.

Topping: In a saucepan, blend the cornstarch and sugar. Add the water and lemon juice and cook over medium heat until the sauce thickens. Add the blueberries and cook an additional 2 minutes. Cool. Spoon cooled blueberry topping over baked squares. Refrigerate until chilled. Serve with fresh whipped cream or other dessert topping. These squares keep best if covered and refrigerated.

Makes 24 squares.

Purple Cow

A favorite for kids of all ages.

2½ cups	milk	625 mL
1⅓ cups	wild blueberries	325 mL
1 tsp	granulated sugar	5 mL

Combine all ingredients in a blender and blend at high speed until smooth.

Makes 3 servings.

Fresh wild blueberries are available from mid-August to mid-September.

WILD BLUEBERRY PIE

This is a new twist on the traditional blueberry pie. The crust is a prebaked shortbread base instead of regular pie pastry. Because the blueberries are added to a cooked blueberry sauce, they retain their shape and firmness. The cornstarch allows the beautiful rich color to shine through.

Blueberries have been dubbed nature's convenience food because they do not need to be cored, peeled or cut to be enjoyed.

1 cup	all-purpose flour	250 mL
2 tbsp	icing sugar	25 mL
½ cup	butter, softened	125 mL
¼ cup	cornstarch	50 mL
pinch	salt	pinch
¼ cup	water	50 mL
1 cup	blueberries	250 mL
¾ cup	granulated sugar	175 mL
½ cup	water	125 mL
3 cups	blueberries	750 mL
½ tsp	lemon juice	2 mL

In a small bowl, blend the flour and icing sugar. Cut in the butter with a fork or pastry blender to form a fine crumb and refrigerate for 30 minutes. Press the chilled dough firmly into the base and up the sides of a 9-inch (23-cm) pie plate. Bake in a preheated 375°F (190°C) oven for 10 to 12 minutes. Cool before adding filling.

In a saucepan, whisk together the cornstarch, salt and ¼ cup (50 mL) water to make a paste. Add the 1 cup (250 mL) blueberries, sugar and ½ cup (125 mL) water, stirring well. Over high heat, bring to a boil, then reduce heat to medium and cook until sauce thickens, stirring constantly. Remove from heat and stir in the 3 cups (750 mL) blueberries and lemon juice. Pour into pie shell and cool. Serve with whipped cream garnished with lemon zest.

Makes 8 servings.

BLUEBERRY CUSTARD PIE

Yogurt not only lightens the custard filling, but in combination with the lemon juice makes a less sweet filling that is a nice alternative to the traditional cream and egg-based version. We use lots of blueberries, which can be either fresh or frozen.

Crust

⅓ cup	butter	75 mL
¼ cup	granulated sugar	50 mL
1	egg	1
1 cup	all-purpose flour	250 mL
½ tsp	baking powder	2 mL

Filling

2	eggs	2
3 tbsp	brown sugar	45 mL
¼ tsp	ground nutmeg	1 mL
¼ tsp	ground cinnamon	1 mL
1 cup	plain yogurt	250 mL
3 tbsp	lemon juice	45 mL
2 cups	blueberries, fresh or frozen	500 mL

Crust: In a small mixing bowl, cream together with an electric hand mixer the butter and sugar. Add the egg and beat until well blended. In a small bowl, blend the flour and baking powder, and add to the creamed ingredients. Stir to make a soft dough. Form the dough into a ball. Wrap dough in wax paper and refrigerate for 1 hour.

Filling: In a mixing bowl, whisk together the eggs, sugar, nutmeg, cinnamon, yogurt and lemon juice until smooth.

Remove the dough from the refrigerator and roll it out on a floured surface to fit a 9-inch (23-cm) pie plate. Line the pie plate with the crust; trim and crimp the edges. Add the blueberries (if using frozen berries, thaw and drain) to the crust-lined pan, then carefully pour the filling over the berries. Bake in a preheated 350°F (180°C) oven for 55 to 60 minutes or until the filling is set.

Allow to cool on a rack and then chill for at least 1 hour before serving

For recipes calling for thawed frozen blueberries, follow these thawing tips:
- *for best results, thaw slowly in the refrigerator*
- *do not use running water to thaw*
- *thawed blueberries will keep covered in the refrigerator for up to 3 days*

Makes 8 servings.

BLUEBERRY CHEESECAKE

This novel no-bake cheesecake has the blueberry sauce as the middle layer, as opposed to the top. It makes for a spectacular dessert that is best prepared a day ahead.

⅓ cup	granulated sugar	75 mL
¼ cup	cornstarch	50 mL
½ cup	water	125 mL
2 tsp	lemon juice	10 mL
2 cups	blueberries, fresh or frozen	500 mL
1½ cups	graham wafer crumbs	375 mL
⅓ cup	butter, melted	75 mL
½ cup	heavy or whipping cream (35%)	125 mL
1 pkg	250 g cream cheese, softened	1 pkg
½ cup	granulated sugar	125 mL
1 tsp	vanilla	5 mL

In a saucepan, blend ⅓ cup (75 mL) sugar and the cornstarch, then add water and lemon juice. Whisk until smooth. Add blueberries. Stirring constantly, bring to a boil and then reduce the heat and simmer until thickened and clear. Cool.

In a small bowl, combine graham wafer crumbs and butter to form a fine crumb. Reserve ⅓ cup (75 mL) for garnish. Press remaining crumb mixture into the bottom of a 9-inch (23-cm) square baking pan or 9-inch (23-cm) springform pan. Chill.

In a small bowl, whip the cream. In another bowl, beat the cream cheese with ½ cup (125 mL) sugar and the vanilla until fluffy. Fold in whipped cream.

To assemble the cheesecake, spread blueberry mixture over the crumb base. Spread the cream cheese mixture evenly over the blueberries. Sprinkle with remaining crumbs. Chill overnight.

Makes 12 to 15 servings.

WILD BLUEBERRY SAUCE

The uses for wild blueberry sauce are limited only by your imagination—it can make a topping for ice cream or yogurt; use it to create a blueberry shortcake, for a cheesecake topping or warmed over pancakes.

⅓ cup	granulated sugar	75 mL
1 tbsp	cornstarch	15 mL
½ cup	water	125 mL
1 tsp	lemon juice	5 mL
1½ cups	blueberries, fresh or frozen	375 mL

In a medium-sized saucepan, combine sugar and cornstarch. Add the water and lemon juice, stirring to combine. Bring to a boil over medium high heat, stirring constantly. Reduce heat and simmer until thick and clear. Add blueberries and simmer an additional 2 minutes.

Cool before serving. May be stored, covered, in the refrigerator for up to 3 weeks.

Makes 1⅔ cups (400 mL).

WILD BLUEBERRY VINAIGRETTE

Many blueberry producers also keep honey bees to assist in pollinating the blueberry blossoms and to get a secondary crop, honey. It might also help explain why wild black bears have been known to travel up to 6 to 9 miles (10 to 15 km) in search of wild blueberries, with perhaps a little honey on the side.

This recipe shows you how to create your own blueberry vinaigrette without needing to buy blueberry vinegar. The cider vinegar and blueberry flavors blend very well, while the green pepper and onion add a nice dimension to the dressing.

½ cup	olive oil	125 mL
¼ cup	cider vinegar	50 mL
1	clove garlic, minced	1
1 tsp	finely chopped green pepper	5 mL
½ tsp	finely chopped onion	2 mL
1 tsp	granulated sugar	5 mL
1 cup	wild blueberries, fresh or frozen (thawed and drained)	250 mL

Put all ingredients in a food processor. Process until they are puréed. Put vinaigrette dressing through a fine sieve. Refrigerate in a covered container.

To serve, spoon 2 to 3 tbsp (25 to 45 mL) of the vinaigrette dressing over mixed greens. Garnish with fresh blueberries and thin apple wedges.

Makes approximately 1½ cups (375 mL).

CHAPTER TEN

THE REST OF THE BERRIES

Blueberries may be Nova Scotia's leading berry crop, but we love our strawberries too. Nova Scotians consume about a gallon (4 L) of strawberries each a year—the most strawberries per capita of any Canadians. Why this is so is a bit of a mystery. Perhaps it has something to do with our relatively short growing season and the fact that a ripe strawberry, sweet and juicy, epitomizes summer. Strawberries were waiting here for the Europeans when they arrived more than 300 years ago, and were well liked by the Mi'kmaqs of our province. These Native Canadians picked the tiny wild strawberries, crushed them, mixed them with meal, and baked the dough to make a rough berry bread, a sort of early strawberry shortcake.

In the nineteenth century, trading ships brought us the hybrid strawberry found everywhere today. The new plant was created by combining the cultivated Chilean and wild Fragaria varieties to produce the plump berry with which we are most familiar.

Many people take advantage of the "U-pick" farms to go out into the fields and fill as many containers as they can. Whether picking from the field or selecting strawberries in the market, it is important to know that, unlike many other fruits, berries do not ripen further after they are picked, so avoid greenish ones. If you do go berry-picking, try to go early in the day. It is then that the ripe strawberries are firmest, making them easier to pick, without crushing the delicate fruit. When you get the berries home, keep them refrigerated in a loosely covered container and don't wash them until you plan to serve. This will keep the berries from getting mushy.

Strawberries, of course, are not the only red berry dear to Nova Scotians. The Maritimes and New England are the world's largest producers of cranberries. Cranberries got their name from the shape of their blossoms, which resemble the head of a crane, hence the name "Crane Berries," or as we know it today, cranberries. Nova Scotia producers cultivated the first cranberry crop in Canada, and by the mid-1800s were shipping to Europe. The berry, known to ward off scurvy with its high concentration of vitamin C, was eaten on board the great sailing vessels.

Cranberries grow in bogs and have traditionally been harvested with a wooden hand scoop still used today. Skilled scoopers are able to harvest 100 pounds (45 kg) of berries in a day (a long, back-breaking one, to be sure). The berry harvest begins in late summer, before the first frost. The frost turns the leaves of the berry plant from green to gold, and the late picking, often under a brilliant blue sky, is called the "red gold harvest." By then the commercial crop has already been harvested, and the remaining berries are picked by local residents for use in winter preserves and compotes.

CRANBERRY APPLE CRISP

A real "comfort" dessert that is easy to make and has an old-style look and texture. Serve this slightly chewy crisp warm, with some whipped cream.

3 cups	unpeeled, chopped apples	750 mL
2 cups	cranberries	500 mL
¾ cup	granulated sugar	175 mL
1½ cups	rolled oats	375 mL
½ cup	brown sugar	125 mL
⅓ cup	all-purpose flour	75 mL
⅓ cup	chopped pecans	75 mL
¼ cup	melted butter	50 mL

In an 8-inch (20-cm) square baking dish, combine apples, cranberries and sugar, and mix thoroughly to blend.

In a small bowl, combine rolled oats, sugar, flour and nuts until well mixed. Add butter and mix with a fork until the mixture forms a coarse crumb. Spread crumb mixture evenly over the fruit. Bake in a preheated 350°F (180°C) oven for 1 hour or until fruit is tender.

Serve hot with whipped cream or ice cream.

Makes 8 servings.

Cranberries offer the last burst of color at the very end of the harvest season. The sea of red berries bobbing up and down in the bogs where they are grown is a grand sight. These are hardy berries, thick-skinned enough to keep in the fridge for up to two months, and frozen for a year. Be sure to toss out the berries that are not bright red and plump.

CRANBERRY AND WILD BLUEBERRY PIE

This is a rare case where we recommend using a canned ingredient (the cranberry sauce). Of course, you can make your own easily enough but a canned variety made of whole berries and sugar will provide equally good results.

⅓ cup	firmly packed brown sugar	75 mL
¼ cup	granulated sugar	50 mL
2 tbsp	all-purpose flour	25 mL
2 tbsp	cornstarch	25 mL
⅛ tsp	salt	0.5 mL
1	14-oz (398-mL) can whole berry cranberry sauce	1
2 tbsp	orange juice	25 mL
½ tsp	grated orange peel	2 mL
2 cups	blueberries, fresh or frozen	500 mL
1	9-inch (23-cm) double pie crust	1
2 tbsp	butter	25 mL

In a mixing bowl, blend the brown and granulated sugars, flour, cornstarch and salt. Stir in the cranberry sauce, orange juice and peel until well combined. Stir in blueberries.

Line a 9-inch (23-cm) pie plate with half of the pie crust. Trim the edge close to the rim of the pan. Spoon in the cranberry and blueberry filling, dot with butter and top with top crust. Trim and seal edges. Cut vents to allow steam to escape.

Bake in a preheated 425°F (220°C) oven for 40 minutes or until crust is golden. Cool to room temperature before serving.

Makes 8 servings.

CRANBERRY OATMEAL MUFFINS

This is an oatmeal-based muffin that we think goes especially well with a cup of dark roasted coffee or cappuccino. Blueberries can very easily be substituted for the cranberries.

1 cup	rolled oats	250 mL
1 cup	buttermilk*	250 mL
¾ cup	brown sugar	175 mL
1	egg	1
¼ cup	vegetable oil	50 mL
1 cup	all-purpose flour	250 mL
½ tsp	salt	2 mL
1 tsp	baking powder	5 mL
½ tsp	baking soda	2 mL
1 cup	cranberries, fresh or frozen	250 mL

*If buttermilk is not available, sour the milk by taking a 1-cup (250-mL) liquid measure and add 2 tbsp (25 mL) of either lemon juice or white vinegar. Add sufficient milk to make 1 cup (250 mL) and stir.

In a mixing bowl, stir together the rolled oats and buttermilk. Add the brown sugar, egg and oil, and stir to mix well. In a small mixing bowl, blend the flour, salt, baking powder and soda. Add to liquid ingredients, stirring to just combine, but do not over-stir. Fold in cranberries. Fill greased muffin tins or cups ¾ full of batter. Bake in a preheated 400°F (200°C) oven for 15 to 20 minutes or until muffins are golden brown.

Makes 12 muffins.

FRESH STRAWBERRY PIE

If using frozen cranberries, take them directly from the freezer. Dust lightly with all-purpose flour. This will help suspend them in the batter and keep them from bleeding—it works with other frozen berries, too.

Big ripe fresh strawberries seem to hold onto the hot summer sun and turn it into something that we can taste. This no-bake pie is a must-make during strawberry season. The glaze holds the pie together and makes the strawberries sparkle like rubies.

3 cups	sliced strawberries	750 mL
1	prebaked single pie crust shell	1
½ cup	granulated sugar	125 mL
2 tbsp	cornstarch	25 mL
1 cup	crushed fresh strawberries	250 mL
⅔ cup	water	175 mL

Arrange the sliced strawberries in the prebaked pie shell. In a saucepan, blend the sugar and cornstarch. Add the crushed strawberries and water. Bring to a boil and stir until thick and clear. Pour over the strawberries in the pie shell. Chill. Serve with whipped cream, garnished with a whole berry and a fresh mint leaf.

Makes 6 to 8 servings.

STRAWBERRY SHORTCAKE

Visitors to Nova Scotia who partake of one of the famous lobster suppers can't leave the table without being offered a big bowl of strawberry shortcake topped with whipped cream. During strawberry season, you will find countless strawberry suppers celebrating the harvest.

Shortcake

2 cups	all-purpose flour	500 mL
4 tsp	baking powder	20 mL
1 tbsp	granulated sugar	15 mL
½ tsp	salt	2 mL
½ cup	shortening or margarine	125 mL
· 1	egg	1
⅓ cup	milk	75 mL
⅓ cup	sour cream	75 mL

In a mixing bowl, combine the flour, baking powder, sugar and salt. Cut in the shortening or margarine until well blended. In a small bowl, beat together the egg, milk and sour cream. Add to the flour mixture, mixing until well blended. Turn onto a floured surface and roll out to 1 inch (2.5 cm) in thickness. Cut into 2-inch (5-cm) rounds. Bake in a preheated 375°F (190°C) oven for 10 to 15 minutes or until golden brown.

Strawberry Topping

4 cups	fresh or frozen strawberries, thawed	1 L
1 cup	granulated sugar	250 mL

Mash the strawberries and stir in the sugar until completely dissolved.

To serve, top warm or cool biscuits with strawberries and top with whipped cream. Garnish with a whole or cut strawberry. Any extra biscuits are delicious with strawberry jam.

Makes 6 to 8 servings.

STRAWBERRY RHUBARB COBBLER

When purchasing fresh strawberries, select only firm, bright red strawberries with vivid green caps.

The two main ingredients, strawberry and rhubarb, are a famous duo, in part no doubt because the sweet strawberry and the tart rhubarb are in season at the same time and the flavors play off each other so well.

2 cups	sliced strawberries	500 mL
3 cups	chopped rhubarb	750 mL
2 tbsp	lemon juice	25 mL
⅔ cup	granulated sugar	150 mL
1 cup	all-purpose flour	250 mL
½ cup	rolled oats	125 mL
2 tsp	baking powder	10 mL
3 tbsp	brown sugar	45 mL
1 tsp	cinnamon	5 mL
1 tsp	lemon rind	5 mL
¼ cup	chopped walnuts	50 mL
⅓ cup	butter	75 mL
1 cup	milk	250 mL

In a mixing bowl, combine strawberries, rhubarb, lemon juice and sugar. Put mixture in the bottom of a 9-inch (23-cm) square baking dish. In a mixing bowl, blend the flour, rolled oats, baking powder, brown sugar, cinnamon, lemon rind and nuts. Cut in the butter with a pastry blender or fork to make a fine crumb. Add the milk and stir to just combine. Drop by spoonfuls on top of the strawberry mixture. Bake in a preheated 400°F (200°C) oven for 35 to 40 minutes.

Makes 6 servings.

PEPPERED STRAWBERRIES WITH WARM ZABAGLIONE

Cracked black pepper brings the strawberry flavor to new heights and makes this simple dessert an elegant finale to a meal.

Rinse the berries just before serving. Remove caps only after washing.

2 cups	fresh strawberries	500 mL
½ to 1 oz	Grand Marnier or brandy	15 to 25 mL
2 tbsp	granulated sugar	25 mL
1 tsp	cracked black pepper	5 mL

Rinse the strawberries. Remove the hulls and cut larger berries in half or quarters. Toss the berries with the Grand Marnier, sugar and black pepper. Refrigerate for 30 minutes.

Zabaglione

4	egg yolks	4
⅓ cup	granulated sugar	75 mL
½ cup	sweet white wine	125 mL

Put the egg yolks, sugar and wine in the top of a double boiler or stainless steel bowl and whisk for 1 minute. Set the top part of the double boiler or steel bowl over a pot of steaming water. Whisk constantly making sure the egg yolks do not curdle. Slowly cook the mixture for 10 minutes or until you have a very creamy consistency and it is very warm to the touch.

Place a small scoop of vanilla ice cream in a parfait glass. Add a quarter of the strawberry mixture to each glass, including some of the syrup. Top with the zabaglione and serve.

Makes 4 servings.

STRAWBERRY BLENDER ICE

Many of us shy away from making homemade ice cream
since most recipes require a special ice-cream maker.
This recipe uses frozen strawberries that actually freeze
the mixture right before your eyes, as it processes. The
low sugar content lets the strawberry flavor
shine through.

3 cups	whole frozen strawberries	750 mL
½ cup	whipping cream	125 mL
2	eggs	2
⅓ cup	granulated sugar	75 mL
2 tsp	lemon juice	10 mL

Remove strawberries from freezer about 5 minutes before starting
the preparation. In a blender or food processor process cream,
eggs and sugar 5 to 10 seconds to blend. With the blender or
processor set at its highest speed, drop in the frozen berries one at
a time. Process until smooth, stopping as required to stir thickening
mixture. Stir in lemon juice.

This tangy soft ice can be served immediately or stored in the
freezer to become firmer. Remove from the freezer 15 to 20 minutes
before serving to soften slightly.

Makes 4 to 5 servings.

Strawberries : Equivalents and Yields:
1 quart box weighs about 1 1/4 lbs (625 g)

1 quart box = 4 cups (1 L) whole berries (fresh)
*   = 3 cups (750 mL) sliced berries*
*   = 2 cups (500 mL) puréed berries*

SHORTBREAD

No Nova Scotia cook with any Scottish roots is without a shortbread recipe. The proportions seem to vary endlessly, and although there are only a few ingredients, the resulting cookie differs from baker to baker. This recipe is so good and simple that there is no reason to buy imported shortbread except to get a pretty tartan tin for your sewing kit.

Shortbread is a traditional Christmas season treat now enjoyed at any time of the year. The key to making authentic shortbread is to use only butter for the shortening.

2 cups	softened butter	500 mL
1 tsp	vanilla extract	5 mL
½ cup	cornstarch	125 mL
1 cup	icing sugar	250 mL
3 cups	all-purpose flour	750 mL

In a mixing bowl, cream the butter with an electric hand mixer until it is light and fluffy. Beat in the vanilla. Add the cornstarch and beat with the mixer until well blended, followed by the icing sugar. Add the flour 1 cup (250 mL) at a time and stir by hand until well blended, resulting in a soft dough. Using manageable portions, place the dough on a floured surface and roll out to ¼ inch (6 mm). Cut into desired shape—round, heart-shaped for Valentines' Day, Christmas shapes, etc. Place on a cookie sheet and bake in a preheated 325°F (160°C) oven for 8 to 10 minutes.

Makes 6 dozen cookies.

BUMBLE BERRY MUFFINS

Both raspberries and blackberries grow on woody stems from 3 to 6 feet (1 to 2 m) tall, which are covered with sharp prickles. The picker of these tasty fruits had best come to this berry patch with long sleeves and pants— and still expect the odd scratch. Each berry is made up of an aggregate of tiny individual fruits or druplets. When the berries are ripe, they easily separate from the white center receptacle and fall off in a thimble-like shape.

This is another old Scottish recipe, "Bumble Berry," an assortment of berries and fruit. Different combinations will work so that the muffins can be made any time throughout the growing season with whatever is fresh at the market. But this recipe is not just a summertime favorite, as frozen fruit works just as well.

2½ cups	all-purpose flour	625 mL
¾ cup	granulated sugar	175 mL
2 tsp	baking powder	10 mL
½ tsp	salt	2 mL
2	eggs	2
¼ cup	melted butter	50 mL
1¼ cups	milk	300 mL
2 cups	assorted berries*	500 mL

raspberries, blackberries, strawberries, blueberries

In a mixing bowl, blend the flour, sugar, baking powder and salt. In a small bowl, beat together the eggs, butter and milk. Stir into the dry ingredients and fold in the berries. Either grease or line muffin tins with paper muffin cups. Spoon the bramble berry batter into each muffin cup, filling three-quarters full. Bake in a preheated 350°F (180°C) oven for 30 to 35 minutes. Turn out onto a wire rack to cool.

Makes 24 small or 18 medium-sized muffins.

Tip: To make this very soft dough easier to handle, cover and chill it in the refrigerator for up to an hour.

CAPE BRETON BUMBLE BERRY TARTS

Our combination of berries and apples in a tart shell is sure to be welcomed at a pot-luck supper or as a welcome-to-the-neighborhood gift.

Pastry

1 cup	softened butter	250 mL
½ cup	icing sugar	125 mL
1	egg yolk	1
1 tsp	vanilla	5 mL
2 cups	all-purpose flour	500 mL
2 tbsp	cornstarch	25 mL
¼ tsp	salt	1 mL

In a mixing bowl, cream butter with sugar until fluffy. Beat in egg yolk and vanilla. In a small bowl, blend the flour, cornstarch and salt. Gradually stir into creamed mixture. Turn out on a lightly floured surface and knead gently. Make ¾-inch (2-cm) balls from the dough and place in 1½-inch (4-cm) tart pan. Gently press evenly over bottom and up sides to form a shell.

Filling and Crumb Topping

½ cup	peeled, chopped apples	125 mL
½ cup	blueberries	125 mL
½ cup	strawberries	125 mL
½ cup	raspberries	125 mL
1 cup	granulated sugar	250 mL
¾ tsp	ground cinnamon	3 mL
¼ cup	cornstarch	50 mL
½ cup	all-purpose flour	125 mL
½ cup	brown sugar	125 mL
½ cup	rolled oats	125 mL
½ tsp	cinnamon	2 mL
¼ cup	butter or margarine	50 mL

In a mixing bowl, gently combine the apples, blueberries, strawberries and raspberries. In another bowl, blend the sugar, cinnamon and cornstarch. Add to fruit mixture and gently toss to coat. Fill the tart shells with the fruit mixture.

In a small bowl, blend the flour, sugar, rolled oats and cinnamon. Cut in the butter with a pastry blender or fork until a fine crumb forms. Top each tart with crumble topping. Bake in a preheated 350°F (180°C) oven for 1 hour or until crumb topping is crisp.

Makes 24 tarts.

RASPBERRY BLUEBERRY GRUNT

Grunt traditionally refers to a blueberry dessert topped with sweet steamed dumplings. Here we combine raspberries with the blueberries for a tasty combination. We have uncovered a couple of theories about the term grunt. One has to do with the sound emitted from the dumplings as they cook, and the other with the sound emitted from the diner after overindulging.

2 cups	wild blueberries, fresh or frozen	500 mL
2 cups	raspberries, fresh or frozen	500 mL
½ tsp	ground nutmeg	2 mL
½ tsp	ground cinnamon	2 mL
¾ cup	granulated sugar	175 mL
1 tbsp	lemon juice	15 mL
½ cup	water	125 mL

Dumplings

2 cups	all-purpose flour	500 mL
4 tsp	baking powder	20 mL
½ tsp	salt	2 mL
1 tbsp	granulated sugar	15 mL
2 tbsp	butter or shortening	25 mL
	Milk	

For stews, pea soup etc. omit sugar, + add water instead of milk. I halved the recipe for 4.

In a large saucepan with a tight-fitting cover, combine the berries, cinnamon, nutmeg, sugar, lemon juice and water. Stir to blend. Boil gently until berries are slightly cooked down.

Dumplings: In a mixing bowl, blend the flour, baking powder, salt and sugar. Cut in butter to form a coarse crumb and add enough milk to make a soft biscuit dough. Drop by spoonfuls into the hot berry sauce. Cover tightly with a lid and simmer for 15 minutes (no peeking!). The dumplings should be puffed and well cooked. Transfer cooked dumplings to serving dish. Ladle sauce over top; serve with whipped cream.

Makes 6 to 8 servings.

RASPBERRY SYLLABUB

Syllabub is first cousin to eggnog, and is a traditional southern dessert for holidays and gala occasions. Syllabub came from England by way of early settlers

1 cup	fresh raspberries or frozen, unsweetened whole, thawed	250 mL
1½ tsp	water	7 mL
¼ cup	white wine	50 mL
½ cup	egg whites	125 mL
1¼ cup	whipping cream	300 mL
¼ cup	icing sugar	50 mL
1 tsp	lemon juice	5 mL

In a saucepan, over medium heat, cook the raspberries and water for 2 to 3 minutes, then set aside in the refrigerator to chill. Remove from the refrigerator and add the white wine to the raspberry mixture. Pass this mixture through a fine sieve to remove the raspberry seeds. In a mixing bowl, whip the egg whites until stiff peaks form. In another bowl, whip the whipping cream, gradually adding the icing sugar. Fold the whipped egg whites into the raspberry mixture and then gently mix in the lemon juice. Fold the whipped cream into the raspberry mixture and gently mix until well combined.

To serve, fill champagne, wine or parfait glasses with the syllabub and cover with plastic wrap. Refrigerate until ready to serve. You may want to top with additional whipped cream.

Makes 6 to 8 servings.

BLACKBERRY APPLE PIE

Big plump blackberries are the woodland and roadside berry sought after by many a hiker or Sunday driver. In combination with a firm baking apple, they create a pie that needs little seasoning beyond a pinch of nutmeg. This recipe works equally well with raspberries.

2 cups	blackberries or raspberries, fresh or frozen	500 mL
2 cups	peeled and sliced apples	500 mL
⅔ cup	sugar	150 mL
½ tsp	ground nutmeg (optional)	2 mL
1 tbsp	all-purpose flour	15 mL
dash	salt	dash
1 tbsp	lemon juice	15 mL
1 tbsp	butter	15 mL
	Pastry for one 9-inch (23-cm) double pie crust	

In a mixing bowl, toss the blackberries or raspberries and apples with the sugar, nutmeg, flour, salt and lemon juice. Line a 9-inch (23-cm) pie plate with bottom crust. Add blackberry-apple filling. Dot with butter. Cover with top crust, and trim and seal edges. Cut vents to allow steam to escape. Bake in a preheated 375°F (190°C) oven for 45 minutes.

Makes 8 servings.

CHAPTER ELEVEN

FROM THE ORCHARD

In 1604, French settlers arrived on Nova Scotia's western coast, bordering the Bay of Fundy. They named their settlement L'Acadie (Acadia), and it became the focal point for the industrious French farming industry that would prosper for more than 100 years, until the political problems with the later-arriving British colonists forced the infamous exile to Quebec and Louisiana. The French farmers found rich soil and a temperate climate similar to that of the great French fruit-growing regions and promptly began planting apple trees. These folks took their apple trees seriously. In fact, a regular tree census was held to determine the success rate of the planters. In 1698 the record books account for 1,548 trees, beginning in the old French settlement of Port Royal, the capital of Acadia, and going up the Annapolis Valley to the north and east of the Fundy coast. Many varieties of apples were planted over the years—over 100, according to a 1950s survey. They range from sweet to tart, good eating to good baking, fragile to sturdy. But the sheer variety only increased the risk of pests and diseases to which apples are susceptible. The Nova Scotia Fruit Growers Association, founded in 1863 to promote the increasingly important fruit crop, encouraged the industry to replant the orchards in the 1970s with fewer varieties that were both popular with the public and more resistant to disease. As a result, most orchards today feature the versatile McIntosh, the excellent pie apples—Spy, Idared and Gravenstein—and the crunchy Cortland. Newer varieties such as Jonagold and Empire have also cropped up over the last twenty years.

Apples should be kept very cool (close to 32°F/0°C), but not frozen. They also need to be stored apart from other fruits, since the naturally occurring ethylene gas emitted from the apple speeds the ripening of other fruit. (This is a fact to remember if you want to ripen some bananas or pears, however. Place the fruit in a paper bag with an apple to shorten the ripening time.) Each apple variety has its own attributes, and those that have the best taste and texture for eating raw are not necessarily the best for baking or for juice. It is very disappointing to spend the time making a flaky pie pastry and preparing the apples and spices only to get a pie that comes out looking like hot applesauce. It is a very good idea to consult the chart we have provided here to determine the best apple for your recipe.

Pears are the other popular orchard fruit in Nova Scotia. The two most popular types are the Clapp Favorite, which ripens into a very yellow, juicy fruit that is great eaten fresh, and the Bartlett, a greenish-yellow pear with a firmer flesh that is good fresh or for cooking. With a little persistence you can also find locally grown bronze Bosc or sweet Anjous. The pear is a fruit that needs to be picked before it is ripe. In fact, the texture and the flavor improves when it is allowed to ripen off the tree, at room temperature.

Nova Scotia Apple Varieties

Select the apple variety that is best suited for its intended use for best results.

Variety	Fresh Salad	Sauce	Pies	Baking
Gravenstein	Good	Excellent	Excellent	Fair
McIntosh	Fair	Good	Fair	Poor
Cortland	Excellent	Very good	Good	Good
Red Delicious	Fair	Poor	Poor	Poor
Spartan	Good	Good	Good	Fair
Northern Spy	Good	Good	Excellent	Excellent
Idared	Good	Good	Excellent	Excellent

APPLE SQUARES

"Tea sweets" is a name given to a large variety of baked squares and tarts. Fruit-filled pastries appear in almost every baker's repertoire. These apple squares remain moist for a couple of days if kept covered, although it is not likely that anyone would take that long to polish off a pan.

Crust

¾ cup	butter, softened	175 mL
1 cup	firmly packed brown sugar	250 mL
1¾ cups	rolled oats	425 mL
1½ cups	all-purpose flour	375 mL
¼ tsp	baking soda	1 mL
	Pinch of salt	

Filling

2½ cups	apples, peeled and sliced	625 mL
2 tbsp	butter	25 mL
¼ cup	pure maple syrup	50 mL
½ tsp	ground cinnamon	2 mL
½ tsp	ground nutmeg	2 mL
1 tsp	lemon juice	5 mL
½ tsp	lemon rind	2 mL

Crust: In a small bowl, using an electric hand mixer, cream together the butter and sugar until smooth. Add the remaining ingredients and stir until well blended.

Spoon two-thirds of the crust mixture into a greased 9-inch (23-cm) square baking pan, pressing the crust mixture firmly into the base of the pan.

Filling: Layer the sliced apples on top of the crust and dot with butter.

In a small bowl, combine maple syrup, cinnamon, nutmeg, lemon juice and rind. Spoon over the apples. Top with the remaining crust mixture. Bake in a preheated 375°F (190°C) oven for 40 to 45 minutes. Apples should be soft and crust browned. Cool in pan and cut into 9 squares and serve warm topped with vanilla ice cream or whipped cream.

Makes 9 servings.

APPLE PEAR BROWN BETTY

Does anyone know the difference between cobblers, crisps and Brown Bettys? Traditionally a cobbler is a baked fruit dessert with a thick biscuit crust. A crisp uses a topping of flour, butter, sugar and spices, and a Brown Betty, usually using apples, is layers of fruit and buttered bread crumbs and sugar.

Using day-old bread as a binder for baked desserts is an old country trick that has recently been rediscovered.

3	large apples	3
3	ripe pears	3
1 tbsp	lemon juice	15 mL
5	slices day old bread	5
¼ cup	melted butter or margarine	50 mL
1 tbsp	pure maple syrup	15 mL
⅔ cup	firmly packed brown sugar	150 mL
½ tsp	grated orange peel	2 mL
¼ tsp	ground cinnamon	1 mL
¼ tsp	allspice	1 mL

Peel and slice apples and pears into thin slices. Place in a bowl, add the lemon juice and toss until well coated. Remove crusts from bread and cut into ½-inch (1-cm) cubes. Put in a bowl and toss with melted butter and maple syrup. In a third bowl, combine brown sugar, orange peel, cinnamon and allspice.

Lightly butter the sides and bottom of a 9-inch (23-cm) square baking pan. Cover the bottom of the pan with one-half of the fruit mixture, followed with one-half of the bread mixture and then one-half of the sugar mixture. Repeat the layering with the remaining ingredients. Cover the pan with foil.

Bake in a preheated 375°F (190°C) oven for 30 minutes. Remove the foil and bake for another 30 minutes. Serve warm with vanilla ice cream or crème anglaise.

Makes 9 servings.

APPLESAUCE CAKE

Prepare this very large cake when you are having a crowd around. But this flavorful cake is also a good keeper and improves with age—it becomes more moist each day.

¾ cup	butter or margarine	175 mL
1 cup	granulated sugar	250 mL
1½ cups	brown sugar	375 mL
2	eggs	2
2½ cups	applesauce	625 mL
¾ cup	grated carrots	175 mL
3 cups	all-purpose flour	750 mL
1½ cups	whole-wheat flour	375 mL
1 tbsp	baking soda	15 mL
½ tsp	ground cinnamon	2 mL
½ tsp	ground nutmeg	2 mL
½ tsp	allspice	2 mL
1½ cups	coarsely chopped walnuts	375 mL
1½ cups	raisins	375 mL

In a large bowl, cream butter until light and fluffy. Gradually beat in the granulated and brown sugars and eggs. In a separate bowl, combine applesauce and carrots. In another bowl, combine the dry ingredients—flours, soda and spices. Alternately add the applesauce and dry ingredients to the butter and sugar mixture until well blended. Fold in the walnuts and raisins. Transfer batter into a greased and floured bundt or tube pan (10 inches/25 cm). Bake at 350°F (180°C) for 1 hour and 30 to 45 minutes or until inserted tester comes out clean and the cake is brown and firm to the touch. Allow to cool for 5 minutes before removing from the pan. Cool completely before icing* and cutting into slices.

The cream cheese icing used with the carrot squares on page 93 is excellent on this cake.

Makes 16 servings.

APPLE DUMPLINGS

The Acadians loved dumpling desserts. These puffy pastries do not completely encase the apple filling but serve as a doughy pillow on which the seasoned fruit sits while baking.

Dumplings

5 to 6	apples	5 to 6
2 cups	all-purpose flour	500 mL
4 tsp	baking powder	20 mL
1 tsp	salt	5 mL
¼ cup	shortening	50 mL
¾ cup	milk	175 mL
⅓ cup	granulated sugar	75 mL
1 tsp	ground cinnamon	5 mL
2 tbsp	butter	25 mL

Topping

2 cups	boiling water	500 mL
1 cup	granulated sugar	250 mL
1 tsp	butter	5 mL
dash	ground cinnamon	dash
dash	ground nutmeg	dash

Prepare apples by peeling and slicing thinly. In a mixing bowl, combine the flour, baking powder and salt. Cut in shortening with a pastry blender or fork to form a coarse crumb. Add milk and stir to form a soft dough. Turn dough out onto a floured surface and roll out into a square to ½-inch (1-cm) thickness. Cut into 8 squares. Place several apple slices on each square. Sprinkle with 2 tsp (10 mL) of granulated sugar, a dash of cinnamon, and dot with butter. Fold in the edges of the dough, pinching corners together to hold in apples. Place in a deep pan or small roaster.

In a mixing bowl, whisk together the water, sugar, butter, cinnamon and nutmeg. Pour over dumplings and bake, covered, in a preheated 350°F (180°C) oven for 45 to 60 minutes.

Serve hot with whipped cream or ice cream.

Makes 8 servings.

CURRIED APPLE CHUTNEY

This quick curried apple condiment complements poultry and other meats.

2 tbsp	butter	25 mL
2 cups	peeled and sliced apples	500 mL
2 tbsp	seedless raisins	25 mL
½ tsp	curry powder	2 mL
pinch	granulated sugar	pinch

In a saucepan, melt the butter over medium heat. Add the apples, raisins, curry powder and sugar and sauté until the apples are tender.

FRESH APPLE COFFEE CAKE

Warm apple cake with its crunchy sweet crumb topping of nuts and cinnamon goes perfectly with a good cup of coffee and lively conversation.

2	eggs	2
½ cup	melted butter	125 mL
⅔ cup	milk	150 mL
2 tsp	grated orange rind	10 mL
2 cups	all-purpose flour	500 mL
2 tsp	baking powder	10 mL
1⅓ cups	granulated sugar	325 mL

Topping

½ cup	chopped almonds	125 mL
¼ cup	lightly packed brown sugar	50 mL
½ tsp	ground cinnamon	2 mL
2¼ cups	coarsely chopped apples	550 mL

In a small bowl, beat the eggs well. Stir in the melted butter, milk and orange rind. In a separate bowl, blend the flour, baking powder and sugar. Make a well in the dry ingredients and add the liquid ingredients all at once, mixing lightly until just combined; do not over-mix. Pour batter into a greased 9-inch (23-cm) square cake pan. Bake in a preheated 350°F (180°C) oven for 15 minutes.

In a small bowl, combine almonds, sugar and cinnamon to form topping. Remove the cake from oven and top with chopped apples and sprinkle with the crumb mixture. Return to oven and bake for an additional 30 to 35 minutes. Serve warm.

Makes 9 to 12 servings.

APPLE BREAD

The pieces of apple keep their shape and texture in this loaf, and with each bite they release some of their moist sweetness. This bread stays fresh for several days if kept wrapped after it has cooled.

½ cup	butter or margarine	125 mL
⅓ cup	granulated white sugar	75 mL
⅓ cup	brown sugar	75 mL
2	eggs, lightly beaten	2
1 tbsp	lemon juice	15 mL
2 cups	all-purpose flour	500 mL
1 tsp	baking powder	5 mL
½ tsp	salt	2 mL
½ tsp	ground cinnamon	2 mL
2 cups	apples, peeled, cored and cut into 1-inch (2.5-cm) pieces	500 mL
1 cup	chopped walnuts (optional)	250 mL

In a mixing bowl, cream together the butter, white and brown sugars, eggs and lemon juice with a hand-held electric mixer. Stir in the flour, baking powder, salt and cinnamon until well combined. Gently mix in the apples and nuts. Pour batter into a greased 9 x 5 inch (23 x 12 cm) loaf pan and bake in a preheated 350°F (180°C) oven for 50 to 60 minutes or until a toothpick inserted into the middle of the bread comes out clean. Turn loaf out of the pan onto a wire rack to cool.

Makes 1 loaf.

Maple Baked Apples

This easy-to-make dessert is one that can be made at the last minute, if the microwave method is used. With only a bit of maple syrup, butter and seasonings, it's a healthy dessert.

4	large apples	4
¼ cup	pure maple syrup	50 mL
¼ cup	chopped dates	50 mL
4 tsp	chopped walnuts	20 mL
4 tsp	softened butter	20 mL
1 tsp	ground cinnamon	5 mL
1 tsp	grated orange rind	5 mL

Wash and core apples. Score apple skin horizontally around the middle to prevent skin from cracking during cooking. Place apples in a baking dish.

In a small bowl, combine maple syrup, dates, nuts, butter, cinnamon and orange rind, stirring well. Evenly spoon the filling mixture into the centers of the four apples. Pour enough water around the apple to prevent sticking. Bake, uncovered, in a preheated 350°F (180°C) oven until apple is tender, between 45 and 60 minutes, occasionally basting with their own juices.

Microwave Method:
Follow instructions as above, placing apples in a microwave-safe dish. Sprinkle with water and cover. Set power on high and cook for 5 to 7 minutes. Let stand for 5 minutes, basting with juices.

Serve warm or chilled.

Makes 4 servings.

ELEGANT APPLE TART

An apple tart is an elegant dessert. Peel and carefully slice the apples in uniform shapes and arrange them in an attractive pattern before baking.

1	9-inch (23-cm) unbaked pie pastry	1
3 cups	unsweetened, chunky applesauce	750 mL
1 tbsp	grated lemon rind	15 mL
1 tsp	vanilla extract	5 mL
pinch	ground cinnamon	pinch
3	medium apples, peeled, cored and thinly sliced	3
¾ cup	apple jelly	175 mL
¼ cup	water	50 mL

Line a deep-dish 9-inch (23-cm) pie plate with pastry. Trim and crimp edges. Bake in a preheated 425°F (220°C) oven for 10 minutes.

In a mixing bowl, combine chunky applesauce (see following recipe) with lemon rind, vanilla and cinnamon. Pour and spread evenly into partially baked crust. Arrange apple slices in overlapping circles on top of applesauce. In a small saucepan, over medium heat, combine apple jelly and water, stirring until jelly is dissolved and smooth. Spread over apple slices. Reduce oven heat to 375°F (190°C) and bake for 30 minutes or until apples are tender. May be served warm with vanilla ice cream or chilled.

Makes 8 servings.

Chunky Applesauce

Roll ⅓ cup (75 mL) grated cheddar cheese into the top crust of an apple pie for extra flavor.

Applesauce is so easy to make—and you can have fun experimenting with the different varieties of apples found on the market. The amount of sugar you use can be varied to suit your tastes. Many people prefer a more tart sauce. We offer you a choice of stove-top or microwave cooking methods.

Stove Top

8	medium-sized apples	8
½ cup	water	125 mL
½ tsp	ground cinnamon	2 mL
1 tbsp	lemon juice	15 mL
½ cup	granulated sugar	125 mL

Peel and slice apples; place in a saucepan. Add water and simmer until apples are soft and break into chunks when stirred. Add cinnamon, lemon juice and sugar, stirring until sugar has dissolved. Serve hot or cold.

Makes 3 cups (750 mL).

Microwave Method

4 cups	peeled and sliced apples	1 L
½ cup	granulated sugar	125 mL
¼ cup	apple juice	50 mL
½ tsp	ground cinnamon	2 mL
2 tsp	lemon juice	10 mL

Combine all ingredients in a microwave-safe bowl. With microwave power set on high, cook covered for 7 to 9 minutes or until apples are soft, stirring once. Remove and stir until apples are chunky.

APPLE PANCAKES WITH CINNAMON SAUCE

Apple pancakes are moist and fragrant. This is the rare time when we suggest forgoing maple syrup in favor of sweet and spicy cinnamon sauce that has its own apple flavor.

To intensify the apple flavor when cooking, replace the water with apple juice or cider.

2 cups	whole-wheat or all-purpose flour	500 mL
¼ cup	granulated sugar	50 mL
1 tsp	salt	5 mL
2	eggs, lightly beaten	2
1½ cups	milk	375 mL
1 cup	finely chopped apples or chunky applesauce	250 mL
1 tsp	vanilla extract	5 mL
1 tbsp	melted butter	15 mL

In a mixing bowl, combine flour, sugar and salt. In a small bowl, mix together the eggs, milk, apples, vanilla and butter until well blended. Gradually add to dry ingredients. Stir until well combined. If the batter appears too dry, add more milk. Drop batter by tablespoonfuls onto a well-greased griddle or skillet and cook until bubbles form on surface. Turn and cook until brown on the other side. Serve hot with cinnamon sauce or maple syrup.

Makes 20 small pancakes.

Cinnamon Sauce

1 cup	brown sugar	250 mL
¾ cup	apple juice	175 mL
½ tsp	ground cinnamon	2 mL
1 cup	chunky applesauce	250 mL
2 tbsp	butter	25 mL

In a saucepan, over medium high, combine sugar, apple juice and cinnamon. Bring to a boil and cook until sauce thickens to a heavy syrup. Add the applesauce and butter, stirring until well combined and butter melts. Serve hot over apple pancakes.

Makes 2 cups (500 mL).

Yields and Equivalents:
Apples

1 lb (500 g)	*= 4 small apples* *= 3 medium apples* *= 2 large apples*
1 medium apple	*= 1 cup (250 mL) diced or sliced apples*
2 medium apples	*= 1 cup (250 mL) grated apples*

Pears

1 lb (500 g) pears	*= 4 small pears* *= 3 medium pears* *= 2 large pears*
1 lb (500 g) pears	*= 1 ½ cups (375 mL) diced pears* *= 2 cups (500 mL) sliced pears* *= 1 cup (250 mL) finely chopped pears*

WINTER SALAD

A wide variety of crunchy apples are available year-round, thanks to advanced storage techniques. As a salad ingredient, they add a refreshing and sweet touch, as does the raw turnip.

2	large tart red apples	2
2 tsp	lemon juice	10 mL
1 cup	shredded turnip	250 mL
1½ cups	sliced celery	375 mL
½ cup	mayonnaise	125 mL
2 tbsp	plain yogurt	25 mL
¼ tsp	salt	1 mL

Dice unpeeled apples and toss with the lemon juice. Combine the apple with the turnip and celery. In a small bowl, whisk together the mayonnaise, yogurt and salt until well blended and smooth. Add to apple mixture, tossing lightly to coat. Chill.

Makes 4 servings.

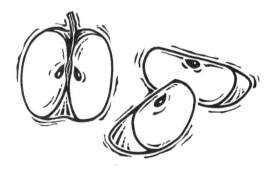

APPLE CUCUMBER RELISH

Relish, put in sterile jars, keeps for a year and makes a fantastic holiday or housewarming gift with a homemade touch that is appreciated by everyone. Try this relish with smoked sausage or turkey.

2 lbs	apples	1 kg
3	cucumbers	3
3	green peppers	3
3	red peppers	3
3	onions	3
1½ tsp	celery seed	7 mL
1½ tsp	salt	7 mL
1½ cups	granulated sugar	375 mL
1½ cups	white vinegar	375 mL
1½ tsp	allspice	7 mL

Peel and core apples. Cut into pieces. Peel and seed cucumbers. Cut into pieces. Cut green and red peppers into pieces, removing seeds and white ribbed sections. Peel onion and cut into wedges. In a food processor, chop the apples, cucumbers, peppers and onion to a relish consistency.

In a large pot, combine the celery seed, salt, sugar, vinegar and allspice. Stir until well blended. Add chopped apple mixture and simmer over low heat for 45 minutes. Put in sterilized jars and seal tightly.

Makes 10 cups (2.5 L).

SPICY PEACH AND TOMATO CHUTNEY

Peaches cooked with savory flavors such as vinegar and ginger are transformed into a striking relish that is marvelous with roasted poultry.

2 cups	peeled and coarsely chopped peaches	500 mL
2½ cups	coarsely chopped, ripe seeded tomatoes	625 mL
½ cup	seedless raisins	125 mL
1 cup	chopped red pepper	250 mL
2 tbsp	finely chopped jalapeño peppers	25 mL
½ cup	chopped onion	125 mL
1 cup	brown sugar	250 mL
¾ cup	granulated sugar	175 mL
¾ cup	white vinegar	175 mL
½ tsp	ground ginger	2 mL
1 tsp	curry powder	5 mL

To make a spicy hot relish, toss ½ cup (125 mL) grated apple with 1 tsp (5 mL) lemon juice; add to ¼ cup (50 mL) horseradish. Serve with pork or beef.

In a large pot, combine all ingredients and let simmer for about 1 hour until thickened. Put in sterilized jars and seal tightly.

Makes 4 cups (1 L).

Caramel Pear Pudding

Pears are certainly overshadowed by apples as the major orchard crop of Nova Scotia. A ripe pear is fragrant and delicious, with a smooth, rich texture. Don't hesitate to buy a pear that is still hard and not ready to eat. This is a fruit that ripens better off the tree. Keep it in a fairly cool spot in the kitchen and refrigerate only when the fruit is ripe.

Grandmother's kitchen comes to mind when we read this recipe. Baked pears have a creamy texture that combines nicely with the crunchy chopped pecans. The caramel-style sauce makes a dessert with a flavor reminiscent of the caramel apples made as special treats at Halloween.

1 cup	all-purpose flour	250 mL
⅔ cup	granulated sugar	150 mL
1½ tsp	baking powder	7 mL
¼ tsp	salt	1 mL
½ tsp	ground cinnamon	5 mL
dash	ground cloves	dash
½ cup	milk	125 mL
2 cups	peeled pears, cut into ½-inch (1-cm) pieces	500 mL
½ cup	chopped pecans	125 mL
¾ cup	brown sugar	175 mL
¼ cup	butter	50 mL
¾ cup	boiling water	175 mL

In a large mixing bowl, combine flour, sugar, baking powder, salt, cinnamon and cloves. Add milk and beat until smooth. Fold in pears and pecans. Turn batter into an 8-cup (2-L) casserole dish.

In a separate bowl, combine brown sugar, butter and boiling water, stirring until the sugar is dissolved and butter melted. Pour evenly over batter. Bake in a preheated 375°F (190°C) oven for 50 to 60 minutes or until knife inserted in center comes out clean. Serve warm with whipped cream or ice cream.

Makes 8 servings.

RECIPE CREDITS

The authors wish to thank the following chefs, member restaurants and individuals for supplying some of the recipes that were used in this book:

Manor Inn (Fruits de Mer, Fettucini au Jardin); Chef Les Dowell (Catch 57); Chef Rob MacIssac (Sautéed Digby Scallops with Honey Onion Chutney, Marinated Mussels, Lamb Shish Kebobs); Kaija Lind, Aqua Prime Mussel Ranch (Tomato Basil Mussels); Chef Claude Aucoin, Pines Resort Hotel (Cream of Asparagus and Oyster Soup, Roasted Purée of Carrot and Zucchini Soup); The Duncreigan Country Inn, Eleanor Mullendore (Grilled Salmon with Dijon Mustard and Honey Marinade, Sole and Salmon Roulades with Dill Sauce, Rosemary Stuffed Leg of Lamb, Herbed Potato Sauté); Chef Alan Johnston, MacAskills (Two-Salmon Tartar); Diane Crowell, Crowell Eel Processing and Smokery (Smoked Mackerel Paté); The Bell Buoy Restaurant (Pan-Fried Haddock with Lemon Butter); Lane's Privateer Inn (Steamed Haddock with Lobster Newburgh Sauce, Brown Bread); Sunshine on Main Cafe and Bistro, Mark Gabrieau (Shark with Tomato and Garlic Sauce, Bruschetta, Peppered Strawberries with Warm Zabaglione); Chef Hans Wicki (Nova Scotia Chicken Stir-Fry, Cream of Chanterelle); The Quarterdeck Beachside Villas and Grill (Grilled Chicken and Spinach Salad, Fried Green Tomatoes, Cinnamon Rhubarb and Pear Crisp, Apple Cucumber Relish, Spicy Peach and Tomato Chutney); Inn on the Lake (Roasted Chicken with Blueberry Peppercorn Sauce); Gwen Johnstone (Tangy Meat Loaf); Chef Don Mailman, Chez la Vigne (Butternut Squash and Carrot Soup); Blomidon Inn (Parsnip and Apple Soup, Raspberry Syllabub); Linda Hatt, Prince's Inlet Bistro (Cabbage with Tangy Mustard Sauce, Rhubarb Relish); Donna Laceby, Amherst Shore Inn (Spinach Soup, Wild Blueberry Vinaigrette); Mrs. Webster, Webster Farms (Mrs. Webster's Baked Beans); Halliburton House Inn (Rhubarb Caramel Pie); Delores Lynds (Rhubarb Squares); Phyllis Cook, Maple Ridge Farms (Maple Pecan Squares, Ruth Smith, Butterscotch Pie); Beth Smith (Blueberry Squares); Lobster Galley, Jean Thiele (Cape Breton Bumble Berry Tarts).

INDEX